P

"People are looking ⸺⸺ ⸺⸺ ⸺⸺ ⸺⸺ ⸺⸺ or the one answer to solve all their problems. This exciting book focuses on small steps . . . many small steps . . . to transform your life."

Elmer L. Towns, cofounder and vice president, Liberty University

"Are you tired, worn down, discouraged, and longing for a vibrant life—a new you? Then this book is the prescription you need. Nelson Searcy and Jennifer Dykes Henson have compiled a simple yet comprehensive list of biblical principles anchored in scientific fact that, when applied, energizes the tired, rejuvenates the worn down, and invigorates the discouraged. Because of God's design for life, if you do what this book teaches, you cannot avoid a healthier and happier life."

Timothy R. Jennings, MD, DFAPA, psychiatrist and author of *The Aging Brain* and *The God-Shaped Brain*

"*The New You* is like a handbook for life. The content is clear, concise, and compelling. And Nelson and Jennifer write in a style that is straightforward, biblical, and highly practical. Your life will be better if you read and do what this book says."

Lance Witt, founder, Replenish Ministries

"Having no vision for your life should be alarming. However, having a big vision with no plan is senseless. This book will help you cultivate both! I love what Nelson and Jennifer have done because they've made complicated concepts incredibly approachable. You're going to want to keep this book near you for the rest of your life."

Clay Scroggins, lead pastor, North Point Community Church

"*The New You* proves a timely book, as Christians are recognizing in increasing number the call to offer our bodies as living sacrifices (Rom. 12:1)."

Matthew C. Easter, assistant professor of Bible, Missouri Baptist University

"The best book in a long time about how to balance spiritual *and* physical health! Searcy and Henson give an easy-to-follow plan for improving health while growing your spiritual life. Keep this book on your nightstand, in your car, or in your bag to consult it often and learn how physical health and spiritual growth were intended to work together."

Bob Whitesel, DMin, PhD, award-winning author
of thirteen books, coach, consultant, and speaker
on church health and growth at ChurchHealth.net

"Progress, not perfection! This approach to life keeps me sane and moving in the right direction. It is also what makes *The New You* such a valuable tool for making the most of your wellness. Read and apply this book and your total person will be transformed!"

Steve Reynolds, pastor of Capital Baptist Church
in Annandale, Virginia, and author
of *Bod4God: Twelve Weeks to Lasting Weight Loss*

"A refreshing and eye-opening read. Their practical and frank confrontation of the questions and unhealthy habits we often have encourages truthful reflection on how we serve as ministers and Christians. This is balanced brilliantly with the small steps to change, which provide motivation and are nonthreatening for persons who can become overwhelmed by just thinking about getting healthy."

Dwight Fletcher, founder and senior pastor,
Transformed Life Church, Kingston, Jamaica

"I was not a healthy pastor. I was overweight, out of shape, stressed out, and headed for an early grave. Two years ago, I finally decided to put into practice the principles that Nelson shares in this book, the same principles that he has been living and sharing with me through coaching. Nelson is right: it really is the small things, done consistently over time, that make a huge impact in every area of life. In the past two years, I've lost over eighty-five pounds and kept it off. I have more energy than I've ever had, and I'm healthier than I've ever been. I cannot wait to share this book with you! You really are one small step away from a brand-new you!"

Pastor Chris Rollins, Coastal Community Church,
Charleston, South Carolina

"Nelson has been my friend and role model for ministry for nearly thirty years. I have witnessed him excel in every area of life, from school to family life to church leadership. The principles that have helped him to be a good friend, husband, father, and pastor are shared in *The New You* in order to take you from an average life to an abundant life."

Michael A. Jordan, pastor, Mount Vernon Baptist Church, Axton, Virginia

"In *The New You*, Nelson and Jennifer not only give the reader a checkup but they also give strategies for improving the most important areas of life. If you desire greater energy, clearer thinking, and spiritual vitality, this is the book for you."

Brian Moore, lead pastor, Crosspointe Church Anaheim

"This book will strengthen your life, regardless of your faith. You will walk away stronger mentally, spiritually, physically, and emotionally. From the first chapter to the last, you will find big and small ideas you can use now. Don't wait; buy this book now."

Jimmy Britt, lead pastor, Rocky River Church, Charlotte, North Carolina

"Nelson and Jennifer have done it again! Having known Nelson for over a decade, I have personally benefited from the teachings in this book. I recommend this book to everyone! And I think it would be a great book for small group study too."

Dr. Rick Mandl, senior pastor, Eagle Rock Baptist Church, Los Angeles, California

"Wholeness and healing are at the top of God's priority list. By clearly explaining the biblical principles that point to full health, the authors make human wholeness not only understandable but, through a series of small steps, doable."

Stan Pegram, lead pastor, BMZ Regional Church

The Generosity Secret

How to Get Out of Debt and Find Financial Freedom

NELSON SEARCY AND
JENNIFER DYKES HENSON

BakerBooks

a division of Baker Publishing Group
Grand Rapids, Michigan

© 2020 by Nelson Searcy

Published by Baker Books
a division of Baker Publishing Group
PO Box 6287, Grand Rapids, MI 49516-6287
www.bakerbooks.com

Printed in the United States of America

Library of Congress Cataloging-in-Publication Data
Names: Searcy, Nelson, author. | Henson, Jennifer Dykes, author.
Title: The generosity secret : how to get out of debt and find financial freedom / Nelson Searcy and Jennifer Dykes Henson.
Description: Grand Rapids, Michigan : Baker Books, a division of Baker Publishing Group, 2020.
Identifiers: LCCN 2020018351 | ISBN 9781540900135 (paperback)
Subjects: LCSH: Generosity—Religious aspects—Christianity. | Christian giving. | Finance, Personal—Religious aspects—Christianity. | Money—Religious aspects—Christianity.
Classification: LCC BV4647.G45 S44 2020 | DDC 241/.68—dc23
LC record available at https://lccn.loc.gov/2020018351

This book contains excerpts from *The Generosity Ladder* by Nelson Searcy with Jennifer Dykes Henson, published by Baker Books in 2010.

20   21   22   23   24   25   26   7   6   5   4   3   2   1

Dedicated to everyone brave enough
to commit to a lifestyle of true generosity.
You are changing the world for the better.

Contents

Acknowledgments   11

Introduction   15

Part 1: The Heart of the Matter

1. Decision Time: *If You Don't Know Where to Start, Start Here*   31

2. A Heart Issue: *How God Sees Your Money*   37

3. Owner versus Manager: *Which One Are You?*   49

4. Just Say No: *What Not to Do with Your Money*   63

Part 2: Breaking Free from Debt for Good

5. Opening Your Hand: *How Generosity Is the First Step in Becoming Debt-Free*   77

6. Down with Debt: *The Three Most Important Financial Decisions You Can Make*   91

Contents

7. Get Out and Stay Out: *A Practical Plan for Showing Debt the Door*   101

8. Capturing the Contentment Thief: *How to Break Free from Materialism*   111

Part 3: Living and Giving Differently

9. Hitting Your Stride: *How to Walk in Step with God's Plan for Your Money*   129

10. The 70 Percent Principle of Lasting Wealth: *How to Set Goals for Giving, Saving, and Investing*   147

11. Living beyond the 70 Percent: *How to Embrace the Full Power of the Generosity Secret*   159

Part 4: Peace, Influence, and Eternal Impact

12. Moving beyond Your Limiting Beliefs: *How to Silence the Misguided Financial Voices in Your Head*   171

13. What Do You Do?: *Trading the Good for the Great in Your Career*   185

14. Putting the Big Rocks in Place: *Five Keys for Embracing the Generosity Secret Now*   197

15. Living for Eternity: *How to Make Sure You and Your Money Have Eternal Impact*   205

A Final Note from Nelson and Jennifer   213

Notes   215

Acknowledgments

Nelson Searcy: The foundation of all I have learned about generosity comes from the first verse I memorized after following Jesus: John 3:16, a reminder that God loved me and the world so much that he gave his utmost. If God is a giver of that magnitude, and if Jesus willingly gave of himself on the cross, then I must also be eager to grow and mature as a giver . . . as a generous person.

In addition to my own biblical study, I have been surrounded by models of generosity, both good and bad. I have seen examples of greed and miserliness and have been nudged by the Spirit to avoid a similar path. Likewise, I have seen examples of amazing generosity, some outlined in this book, and felt compelled by the Spirit to follow a similar path. My own life of generosity is a work in progress, but I am grateful for the Spirit's ongoing guidance.

More practically, I must express my generous appreciation to Jennifer Dykes Henson, my writing partner for over a dozen books. Her commitment to generously share her gifts and talents completely, fully, and amazingly on every page of this book is obvious and appreciated. I have seen up close how she, her husband, Brian, and their amazing family model the principles in this book. Jennifer, thank you!

I would also like to thank some dear personal friends and colleagues for their ongoing generous encouragement and accountability in my life. There are too many to mention, but let me highlight a few: Jimmy Britt, Michael Jordan, Kerrick Thomas, and Jason Hatley. I must also express my appreciation for the privilege I have to work with the incredible team of pastors, leaders, and artists at the two great ministries that occupy my time outside of writing: The Journey Church and Church Leader Insights.

Second only to the eternal gift that God gave me of his Son, Jesus Christ, is the gift of my family. My wife, Kelley, has been beside me during each step of our generosity journey outlined in this book. Together, we know the blessings of generosity. And more so than I, she shares generously and selflessly with our family, friends, and church members. As we approach thirty years of marriage (boy, were we young when we met!), I am more and more grateful she said yes to our first date (a true blind date, but that's for another book). As my son has entered his teen years, I have been encouraged by his growing heart and pull toward generosity. His world is one that is bathed in entitlement, and we work hard to protect him from those inherent evils, but he also does his part. He is generous with his time, care of others, friendship, and his earned income. Alexander, I am proud of you! Thank you for being generous with me when I ask a million questions about your latest video game adventures. (And, by the way, an early congratulations on achieving your black belt in karate . . . the final test for the belt coincides with the release date of this book).

It has once again been a pleasure to work with the fine folks at Baker—many of them new to me and my projects. I appreciate their warm welcome, fast friendship, and highest commitment. My primary contact from the beginning of this book was Brian Vos. In fact, it was the urging of Brian Vos that brought this book into existence—so, Brian, thank you! Thank you for your love for books, for authors, and even for your Detroit Lions. Beyond Brian, thank you to everyone in acquisitions, editorial, publishing, and especially the frontline sales team. You all have my deepest appreciation!

Jennifer Dykes Henson: My partnership with Nelson Searcy over the last fifteen years has been nothing short of incredible. I am continually humbled and grateful to be part of the exciting, eternity-shifting work God has called us into together. Nelson, thank you for inviting me to The Journey–Manhattan offices for that first meeting so many years ago and for all the ways you've encouraged our partnership to grow and evolve since. Each year of writing, and each book, is a great new adventure.

Thank you to my husband, Brian, for being a constant source of love and encouragement and for continually challenging me to live a life worthy of the work I've been called to. And to my two young daughters, Isabelle and Ivey-Grace, my life's goal is to engage in the world in a way that will make you proud and that will model for you the richness of life Jesus offers us all. You are my inspiration.

Finally, thanks to God for once again giving me the opportunity to engage in meaningful work that will, hopefully and prayerfully, influence for the better the lives of those who find it in their hands.

Introduction

When I (Nelson) was in my early thirties, I looked around and realized I was in a big debt hole. Like many of my peers, I had taken out loans to get myself through college and graduate school. My wife, Kelley, and I had married at a young age and made some foolish mistakes. We went on a few vacations we couldn't afford. We got easy credit and bought things we didn't need for our house. After about five or six years of marriage, we had amassed over $22,000 worth of credit card debt, not to mention our outstanding educational debt.

At first, young and naïve as I was, I thought, *Okay, there are a lot of people in this boat. It's not that big of a deal. I can just make the minimum payments on the credit cards, and we'll get them paid off.* Our minimum payment was about $350 per month, which was doable on our new grown-up salaries. The only problem was that after making those payments for about three years, we were still $22,000 in debt. I was doing what I knew to do, but our situation wasn't getting any better.

Shortly thereafter, God threw us a curveball. Kelley and I found ourselves moving to New York City—one of the most expensive places in the world to live—to start a brand-new church. We settled into our pricey (they all are!) Manhattan apartment with less money and less economic security than we had ever had. And that's when God really began to work in my financial life . . . I'll save the rest of the story for the pages ahead.

If you have picked up this book, I bet you can relate to my early financial situation on some level. You are probably looking for an improvement when it comes to your money; perhaps you'd even go so far as to say you're looking for a financial transformation. Maybe you are staggering under the weight of your own debt, and you want to break free. Maybe you want to make more money, learn how to hold on to what you do have, or even discover how to use the almighty dollar as a tool for greater good. Whatever it is you want to improve about your money situation, we're glad you're here.

> How you view and use money will shape the life you live, the impact you have, and the legacy you leave.

We don't have all the answers, but we do have insight into some powerful principles, backed by ancient truths, that can put you on the path to financial freedom. We are not financial advisors; in fact, we'll probably irritate those who are. But in working with people just like you all around the country and the world, we have seen firsthand the power money holds to direct the course of your life. How you view and use money will shape the life you live, the impact you have, and the legacy you leave.

But we're getting ahead of ourselves. Before we dive in, let's spend a few minutes simply thinking about how we see money.

Shifting Perspectives

Have you ever experienced a paradigm shift? You know, a moment of clarity when you realize that there's an entirely different way of seeing things than the way you've always seen them? A fundamental change in perspective that alters your entire approach to the world?

The first step in experiencing a paradigm shift is acknowledging that you see the world through a certain set of lenses. These lenses have been created by many factors—your family, your upbringing, your education, and your social circle, to name a few. Based on your life experience to this point, you engage with the world in a specific way. Or as Shakespeare once wrote, "Such as we are made of, such we be." We would take the liberty to add, "and such we see," to the great writer's assertion. We don't think he'd mind.

The concept of a paradigm shift first came on the scene over half a century ago with Thomas Kuhn's work, *The Structure of Scientific Revolutions*. Kuhn exposed the reality that nearly every important advancement in science is, at its core, a break with an old way of seeing the world—a break with an old paradigm. His revelation proved that to make strides toward any kind of real change, we must first recognize our current paradigms and then open ourselves up to the possibility of a new way of thinking.

Maybe the best way to illustrate this phenomenon is with an actual illustration. Take a look at the image below.

What Do You See?

Depending on your perspective, you may see a beautiful young woman shyly turning her face away from the artist. Or you may see a hunched old woman with a large nose and a downcast gaze. Which woman do you see? Whichever one it is, another reality exists.

If you see the young woman in the picture, we have news for you: this is a picture of an old woman. But to see her, you have to shift your perspective. Here are a few clues to help you see things a different way.

The young woman's ear is the older woman's eye. The curve of her chin is the tip of the old woman's nose. Do you see her yet? One more hint—the choker necklace around the younger subject's neck is the opening of the old woman's mouth. (If you first saw the older woman, just work backward from these clues until you see the younger woman's image.)

Pretty amazing, huh? People actually get angry with one another over this exercise. Sometimes those who see the old woman first are so convinced they are right that they think those seeing something else are crazy. And vice versa. We all tend to think that we see things as they really are, but, obviously, that's not always the case. When we open our minds to a new way of viewing the world, we give ourselves the opportunity to experience life-changing, growth-spurring paradigm shifts.

The Old View versus the New View

Most of us have grown up with a skewed understanding of money and possessions. Based on misinformation from the world around us, poor examples, and our own desires, we have unconsciously developed a certain paradigm for understanding and managing our income, from the first five-dollar bill we were given in a birthday card to our first paycheck, and everything we've received since. Unfortunately for most of us, our financial paradigm has gotten us in trouble. And it's not entirely our fault. We have unwittingly bought into the world's distorted paradigm—a paradigm that has led us into catastrophic debt, broken apart our families, and caused high levels of stress and anxiety.

Even though the majority of us are incredibly wealthy by the world's standards, we are locked in a battle with money. Don't think you are wealthy? Think about this: most of the world's population lives on less than two dollars per day. Read that again. Could you imagine living on two dollars per day? Yet even in our inarguable abundance, most of us have internalized the "buy more now, pay later" mantra of our culture. We have accepted false common views on money management. We've bought into the conventional wisdom that does nothing but cause us problems. No matter how much we have, we always seem to need more. Financial stress is a shadow that never leaves us alone.

Most of our money problems boil down to bad financial decisions—financial decisions that are the result of our distorted perspective, or our incorrect paradigm, of this currency that is so apt to control our lives. In fact, we are usually so rooted in our own paradigm of money management that we don't even realize we are making poor decisions. Like fish in water, we can't see the environment consuming us. We are just doing what we know to do and wondering why we continually live under the thumb of financial oppression.

In order to get back on the right track, we need a good dose of self-examination. Take a look at your own financial life. Here are a few signs that you've been handling money according to the world's prevailing paradigm:

- Your debt is growing each month.
- You have to pay regular living expenses with a credit card.
- You are making only the minimum monthly payments to your creditors.
- You are upside down in your mortgage.
- If you miss one paycheck, you can't cover your bills.
- You and your spouse fight about money regularly. (Money problems are cited as the number-one cause for divorce in America.)

- You are not able to put money into a savings or retirement account every month.
- You are constantly stressed about money.
- You can't give to needs you see around you.
- You are unable to tithe or support your local church.
- You can't go on that vacation you want to go on without adding to your debt.
- You don't know how you are going to pay for your or your child's education, sports gear, health expenses, etc.
- You feel like you don't have the money to live the life you were created to live.

Can you relate to any of these warning signs? If you are like most people we've worked with—heck, most people we've ever met—you can relate to practically all of them.

This is the trap the world's way of thinking has lured us into. Financial strain is not the exception; it's the common story. When we play the game the world has set before us, we lose every time. Handling money the conventional way doesn't work. Operating out of the prevailing mindset lands us in loads of debt and discouragement, bound by money-colored handcuffs. There's no question, the paradigm we've been handed is faulty.

Are you ready for some good news? There is a better way of doing things. A new paradigm is available for your financial life—one that leads to peace, contentment, financial security, and the ability to use your money in ways that bring joy to you and those around you. The old way of handling money falls very short of the promises it makes. There is a better way, a new way. It's there and waiting. You just have to open your eyes to it.

What's God Got to Do with It?

When Jesus stepped onto the scene over two thousand years ago, he introduced a new paradigm to the world. He made all things new—yes, even the way we see and use the currency that's necessary for us to do business, buy food, and put shelter over our heads on this earth. If you know much about Jesus, you know that during his earthly ministry, he often used parables to get his points across. These parables were his tools for shining light on the hidden ways to do things that were better than how people were doing them. And when it comes to money, there is a hidden, better way to do things that he wants us to know about: his way.

As Jesus said, the truth will set you free. And God offers us a lot of truth about how to handle finances in a way that brings peace rather than stress, contentment rather than grasping, and joy rather than desperation. A new, correct perspective on God's plan and purpose for our money is a game changer, as we will explore in detail in the pages ahead. Everything people have tried outside of God's plan for money hasn't worked. We've tried playing by the world's rules, and so have you. Those rules have not gotten us where we want to go. But God, through Jesus, has called us all to something better and given us an outline for how to get there.

History tells us that during his years of ministry, Jesus talked more about money than about heaven or hell. He knew what a big issue this was and would continue to be for all of us, so he spoke into the chaos. In the chapters to come, we'll discover why he was so concerned with money and how the wisdom he offered about personal finances is both radically countercultural and incredibly wise. We're about to give you the secret to Jesus's hidden ways to achieve financial peace. But first, we need to ask you to do three things:

1. Acknowledge that your current way of viewing and managing your money isn't getting you where you want to be financially.
2. Commit to questioning your own paradigm and beginning to see your financial life through a different lens.
3. Choose to be open to the big secret about generosity we are about to expose and to how it can transform your financial reality if you are willing to make the small shifts it requires.

Like all breakthroughs, financial peace begins with a paradigm shift. Just as our old woman's eye was actually the young girl's ear, the dollar bills in your bank account can and need to be looked at from a different perspective.

Perhaps right now, you feel like your money has control over you. That's because your paradigm is giving it control. Perhaps you are convinced that you'll never have enough. That's because your paradigm has led you to this false belief. Maybe you are so far in debt that you can't see a way out. Your paradigm got you there. You may be thinking, *No, my low income got me there*, or *My high cost of living got me there*. We would argue that both of those things, and everything else that can be blamed for a poor financial situation, are an outgrowth of your paradigm—a paradigm handed to you by a system not working in your favor.

As we've worked with hundreds of individuals and couples over the years—from those starting their first real job to those close to retirement—we've constantly heard similar refrains. They all say that the accepted truths society has taught them about money just aren't working. Culture's way of financial management has landed them in loads of debt and left them shouldering the burden of constant financial stress. It's not that there's a shortage of information out there. Browse any bookseller's list and you'll find plenty of bestselling books about money whose advice tens of thousands of people have tried to follow, but those people have ended up failing again and again. Why? The information is faulty. Not only is it steeped in a system not working in your favor, its heartbeat is a pull toward greed that appeals to your most base human nature. You were not created to succeed and find significance through a paradigm built on greed.

Think about it: Almost all popular financial books put forth some variation of "save one hundred dollars" as a first step. Why start there? While at first it may seem reasonable—and yes, we do believe in saving—this first step subconsciously appeals to innate greed. Its strength comes from your fear of not having enough: *I want more. I need more. I must save more . . . starting with this first hundred dollars.* But when you choose to operate out of the greed mindset that society constantly and ruthlessly forces on you, you get the same results that the majority of people in our society are getting: more credit card debt, insurmountable student loans, mortgages that are too high, less savings, skinny investments, and on the list goes. In America today,

- 50% of households live paycheck to paycheck
- 31% have less than $500 in emergency savings
- 62% carry unpaid credit card debt
- 28% default on their student loans
- 30% have no retirement savings[1]

You were created to operate out of a different paradigm. Even though you've grown up in a system that has handed you a skewed set of rules, and even though it may be part of your flesh nature (more on that later) to buy in to those rules, you weren't created to live under constant financial stress. You weren't created to be obsessed with getting, acquiring, or keeping up with what others have. You were created for more. You were created to walk in peace, to have the ability to care for your own needs and help others without struggling to make ends meet month to month.

What if the financial framework you've always accepted as reality is wrong? What if there is a secret way to financial health, security, and freedom—a way that has been hidden in plain sight like the young woman (or the old woman) in that paradigm-shifting picture above? Here's a transformational truth we want you to take hold of: you were created for generosity. Let that sink in. You were *created* for *generosity*. And that generosity is key to your financial freedom as we will explore in the pages ahead. Please indulge us if for no other reason than you know that nothing else you've ever read about financial freedom really works. There is a better way.

When you shift your perspective to a new way of thinking— God's way of thinking—you will experience a financial transformation. But the key is to allow yourself to begin to see your money in a different light. As you read through this guide, stay open to the ideas we present. You will have to step into some uncomfortable territory. There's always tension in transformation. When you've been operating by one set of beliefs for a long time, it can be hard to open yourself up to a new set. But just remember, doing more of what you've always done will only get you more of what you've always gotten. The old way doesn't work; the new way leads to freedom.

Welcome to Your New Financial Reality

Dream with me for a moment. Imagine the following as a reality:

- All of your debt is paid off.
- You don't worry about running out of money before your next paycheck.
- You aren't tempted to buy things you can't afford.
- Your needs are consistently met.
- You have the ability to save for your children's education and your retirement.
- You can go on vacation without going into debt.
- You have the desire and ability to give to people who need help.
- You can go on that mission trip you've always wanted to go on.
- You are able to fully support your local church in God-honoring ways.

- You have the margin to be able to support causes you believe in.
- You live a life full of joy and peace.

The principles contained in the pages ahead have the potential to turn each one of those visions into a reality. Whether or not they will depends on what you decide to do with them.

Here's what we can guarantee: If you will apply what you're about to discover—if you will acknowledge and lean into the new paradigm—you will experience life as you've never known it before. You will finally be able to replace your financial stress with financial freedom. You will be free to live the life you've been created to live, without the weight of constant worry. But you have to be willing to let the new lens of truth clarify your perspective. You have to be willing to shift. Are you ready?

Part 1

The Heart of the Matter

Decision Time

If You Don't Know Where to Start, Start Here

Owe nothing to anyone—except for your obligation to love one another. If you love your neighbor, you will fulfill the requirements of God's law.

Romans 13:8

Everything in life begins with a decision. Think for a moment about all of the decisions you have already made to get where you are right this minute. Last night, you decided what time to set your alarm. This morning, you decided whether or not to hit snooze. You decided what to wear when you got up, what to have for breakfast, and how to interact with the other people in your household. You chose how you feel today. Yes, really. Whether you realize it or not, your emotional state and much of your physical state is a choice, even if a subconscious one. You chose your outlook for the day. You chose how to engage with the things on your to-do list. You chose to pick up this book.

Every single day, we all make hundreds if not thousands of decisions, big and small. These decisions direct the course of each hour, each day, each month, each year of our lives. The decisions we make determine our paths. Maybe the financial decisions you have made have put you on a path you don't feel good about. Thankfully, you're not stuck. You can make the decision to step onto another path. You can break free from the financial strongholds that keep you down. But that begins with—you guessed it—one very important decision.

The Best Financial Decision You Can Make

If you chose this book because you feel like you are drowning financially, you are not alone. Millions of Americans are under extreme financial pressure. Credit cards—not to mention student loan debt, car loans, personal loans, balloon mortgages, and the list goes on—have put many of us in a pit that seems almost impossible to climb out of. As a society, we are not running on Dunkin'; we are running on debt, even as we stagger under its enormous weight.

Why are we okay with living in such a state? Because living in debt has become the widely accepted way to live. Everyone is doing it. After all, isn't debt necessary to maintain a lifestyle that keeps up with the family next door, the mom in front of you in the school pickup line, the guy at the office with the expensive suit and latest phone? (Wait, didn't that phone just release last week?) Of course you have student loans and a car payment. Who doesn't? That's just the way it is. Who could possibly fund the kind of life we all want to live by paying cash? Credit is how you get there, right? Wrong. Credit is the world's answer to contentment, but as everyone who has found themselves in debt comes to realize, there is no contentment in it at all. It is a burden that crushes the soul and causes crippling stress in the long run. And it's the direct result of living within a skewed paradigm.

If you can relate, you've come to the right place. As we get started on this journey toward financial well-being, we want to invite you to begin by making one big, bold, counter-cultural decision—a decision that will likely set you apart from your friends, coworkers, and family members but that will allow you to begin living a life of financial health and peace. This is the place to start if you don't know where else to start. This one decision can begin to turn the tide on your financial stress. If you haven't guessed it by now, here's what we are imploring you to do:

Decide to get out of debt!

Everything begins with a decision, and your journey to financial freedom is no different. Make the decision today that you are not going to live at the mercy of debt and high-interest payments anymore.

Getting Started

Now, as part of that decision, we are going to ask you to do something a little unusual. This is the interactive part of the book, and we hope you'll play along with us. In the chapters to come, we'll further explain the significance of what we are about to ask you to do, but for now, just follow the steps we're about to lay out. Trust us. You'll be glad you did. (If you are already debt-free, that's great! You can skip ahead to chapter 2.)

Step 1: Get a fifty-dollar bill.

Over the next two or three weeks, do whatever you need to do (that's legal!) to get your hands on a fifty-dollar bill. You could sell something online, take your lunch to work instead of eating out, skip the coffee shop, cash in those two-dollar bills you've been saving since you were a kid . . . whatever you need to do, find a way to get a nice, crisp fifty-dollar bill. For some of you this may be easy. Maybe all you need to do is swing through the bank. For others, it will take some creativity. Do what you need to do to make it happen.

Step 2: Cut out a two-inch paper heart.

Find a piece of paper and draw a heart that's about two inches tall. Then cut that heart out. Now attach the paper heart to the front of your fifty-dollar bill. You can use a paper clip, a small piece of tape, or whatever works for you.

As we'll dive into in the next chapter, God sees money as an issue of the heart. If you're ever going to step into a right relationship with money, you have to begin to understand its connection to your heart. Hopefully this visual aid will help.

Step 3: Give yourself a deadline for getting out of debt, and write that date on the front of the paper heart.

On faith, as you make the decision to get out of debt, write down the date by which you'd like to make that happen. If you're having trouble coming up with a date, try thinking about how much money you owe. Calculate how long it would take you to pay off that amount if you started throwing 5–10 percent of your income at your debt every month. Now decide to get out of debt in half the amount of time you just calculated. Whatever that date is, write it on the front of your paper heart.

Step 4: Put your fifty-dollar bill / paper heart where you will see it every day.

You aren't going to do anything with this fifty-dollar bill anytime soon. It's not to spend. You aren't paying down debt with it. You aren't putting it in your savings account. That's what the other books will tell you to do. Rather, it's a tool, a symbol of your evolving relationship with money. Where can you place it that you'll see it every day as a reminder of the decision you've made to get out of debt and of the financial freedom you are working toward? Maybe you tape it to your bathroom mirror, use a magnet to stick it on your refrigerator, or thumbtack it to a corkboard in your office. Wherever it is, pick a place where you will be reminded daily—even several times a day—that you are trading in your old financial paradigm for a new path of financial peace.

If you are struggling to make ends meet and you don't know how to begin climbing out of the hole you've found yourself in, this is your starting point. If you feel like you can't do anything else, just play along with what we've asked you to do in this chapter, and keep reading.

The decision to get out of debt is a life-changing decision. Congratulations on making it. You are one major step closer to living a life of financial well-being.

CHAPTER 2

A Heart Issue

How God Sees Your Money

Wherever your treasure is, there the desires of your heart will also be.

Matthew 6:21

The connection between your heart and your money is complicated. That's because money is not just a financial issue; it's also a spiritual issue. How you view and manage your money impacts you on a spiritual level. Think about that fifty-dollar bill and two-inch paper heart we asked you to create in the last chapter. In the same way that they are tacked together, your financial life and your spiritual life are inextricably bound—which is why your money matters so much to the God who created you.

As we've already mentioned, Jesus himself talked more about money during his earthly ministry than he did about heaven or hell. And as part of that, he confirmed that there's a direct link between your money and your heart (Matt. 6:21). Wherever your money goes, your heart will follow. And since God is primarily concerned with having access to your heart, it only makes sense that he is concerned about what you do with your money. Until you put money in its proper place and begin to handle it in a way that God can honor and bless, your heart will never be able to be fully committed to him and his purposes.

Monkeying Around

You may have heard the famous anecdote about how they catch monkeys in India. Long ago, an insightful hunter figured out that monkeys are selfish little creatures, so he created a method of capture that takes advantage of that nature.

First, the monkey hunter cuts a small hole in one end of a coconut—a hole just big enough for the monkey to fit his hand into—and ties a long cord to the other end. Then, he sprinkles peanuts, banana chunks, or some other enticing treat into the hole, places it in the monkey's path, and sneaks away holding the other end of the cord to watch his plan unfold.

Inevitably, an unsuspecting monkey comes along, sniffs out the treat, inspects the "container," and then wriggles his little hand into the hole to grab the treasure. With that, the hunter's job is done. All he has to do is yank his end of the cord and the whole monkey/coconut kit and caboodle lands at his feet.

But isn't there something missing here? Why wouldn't the monkey just pull his hand out of the coconut and run for his life? Remember that monkeys are selfish. Once they get their hands on something they want, they won't let go. Sound familiar?

With his fist wrapped around the goods, the monkey can't get his hand back out of the hole. If he would just loosen his grip and let go of the bounty, he could save himself. But he clings tightfisted to what's "his" and finds himself ensnared . . . even unto his own demise.

It's easy for us to see how ridiculous the monkey is being. If we were sitting at the edge of the jungle watching the scenario play out, we would be screaming, "Let go! That little fortune isn't worth your life!" And yet, back in our own corner of the world, we are as guilty as the monkey. We hold on too tightly. We want what is ours, and we want it so badly that we are often blind to the consequences of our grasping.

We are born keen on self-preservation and self-promotion. We are all prone to approach life with an almost primal hoarding mentality. We want to be secure. We want to get all we can. We are focused so intently on our treasure that we don't see the hunter lurking behind that nearby tree . . . and therein lies the problem.

What Is the Generosity Secret?

In the case of those monkeys, greed ends up being the defining characteristic of their little lives. Their innate bent toward selfishness skews their view of the world around them, making acquisition of the goods in that coconut more important than anything else. And that selfishness lands them in a heap of trouble. You and I are not so different, are we? The world's paradigm for managing money, which has crippled so many, is a direct outgrowth of humanity's selfish nature.

We are all born selfish. Those of you with kids have witnessed the early displays of selfishness firsthand. As soon as children can talk, *mine* becomes one of their favorite words. Sharing is a concept that parents since the beginning of time have tried to teach early and teach well—and why is it so difficult? Because of every person's innately selfish nature.

I (Jennifer) have two young girls born fourteen months apart. Teaching sharing is a full-time job in our house. Every year around birthday time, this issue raises itself anew. I remember one year in particular, when my oldest was turning five and my youngest was three. This was the first year we had a "friend" birthday party rather than celebrating with just family. That meant a lot more birthday presents than usual. Watching my daughter open those presents was such a joy. She was wowed and grateful for every new treasure—and every one of them became immediately and uncompromisingly hers, of course.

The problem came when my three-year-old would innocently (or not so innocently) grab one of those new toys to look at or play with. Fireworks. That inborn selfish nature reared its head as my older daughter tried to hold on to and protect what was rightfully hers. Then, when my younger daughter's birthday rolled around a few months later, the same scenario played out but with the roles reversed. My children are not unique in this. It's the human condition. Despite the teaching, training, and modeling, those selfish natures are very real—and they need a cure.

Could it be that the reason you are in the financial situation you're in is because your relationship with money and things is still an awful lot like a five-year-old protecting her birthday presents? Your parents may have taught you to think of others and to share, and you may have eventually learned the lesson, as we all do, but deep down there's still a little voice screaming "*Mine!*" A voice that is only bolstered by the overarching financial paradigm you've been taught to operate within. None of us comes into the world with a generous heart. It's something that has to be taught, yes. But even beyond that, we would argue it has to be given to us as we surrender ourselves and our things to God. Generosity is something God can create in all of us as we allow him to replace our selfish nature with his nature of generosity.

You may not think of yourself as greedy—greed is easy to see in others but extremely hard to see in the mirror—but it's inherent personal and cumulative greed that has created the problematic financial paradigm you are living in. A cultural system built on a faulty premise has been the catalyst for the situation you find yourself in. You are struggling financially because of a proclivity toward the abuse of money, which is driven by greed. But God loves you too much to let you stay in that place. He wants to teach you the antidote to greed that can change your life forever. He wants to show you the secret for turning things around. That secret is generosity.

In the end, your life will be defined by either greed or generosity. To be open to the Generosity Secret is to choose to be open to God's way of viewing and handling money, ensuring your ability to live a life of financial freedom that is ultimately defined by generosity. As we've taught the principles in this book to hundreds of people skeptical about God and church, over and over we've heard what might be summarized this way: *Well, I've tried everything else and it didn't work; let me at least give God's way a chance.* And they are always glad they did. That's what we are asking of you; we are asking you to give God's way a chance, whether you are someone who considers yourself a God person or not. No matter where you are starting from, financially or spiritually speaking, this is your open door to freedom.

The Generosity Secret is that generosity is the secret. When you choose to be generous, you interrupt the cycle of selfishness that leads to financial strain. We will unpack everything that assertion means in the pages to come. As part of building out what the Generosity Secret looks like in your life, we will present a collection of smaller practical generosity secrets—subsecrets, if you will—at the beginning of each remaining chapter (plus a few extras scattered throughout) that, when taken together and taken to heart, will help to move you from your current situation to a life of financial freedom and peace. Think of these rubber-meets-the-road generosity secrets as tips or small steps for fully integrating the truth of the Generosity Secret into your life.

> The Generosity Secret is that generosity is the secret.

The Freedom of Openhanded Living

Now, let's put Jesus's declaration about the connection between our heart and our treasure into context:

> Don't store up treasures here on earth, where moths eat them and rust destroys them, and where thieves break in and steal. Store your treasures in heaven, where moths and rust cannot destroy, and thieves do not break in and steal. Wherever

your treasure is, there the desires of your heart will also be. (Matt. 6:19–21)

If we are intent on storing up wealth for ourselves on earth, we will be acting scarily like our primate friends. We will be trading something of eternal value (treasure in heaven) for something that is ultimately of little value (treasures on earth). And as our greedy little hands stay closed over our earthly treasures, that's where our hearts will be fully anchored. We all know what accompanies a life in which money is our top priority . . . stress, lack, and anxiety. All the things we have too much of already.

Here's some great news: you don't have to be afraid of opening your hand and inviting God into your financial life. There is nothing more freeing than acknowledging the truth that your money and possessions are not yours anyway and accepting your role as a manager or steward, as we'll explore in detail in the next chapter. Changing your paradigm will truly change your life.

> It is impossible to become a fully developing follower of Jesus without also becoming a fully developing steward of your financial resources.

The reason so few of us have invited God into our finances is because we haven't been taught to. We don't understand the importance. People in positions of leadership have long been afraid to broach the subject of personal finances, which has left everyone else confused. But without learning how to manage our resources the way God intends, we'll never be able to live the life God created us to live. As one author

noted, "If Christ is not Lord over our money and possessions, then he is not our Lord."[1] In fact, as we contend and
will explore in the pages ahead, it is impossible to become
a fully developing follower of Jesus without also becoming
a fully developing steward of your financial resources. The
truth about money needs to be brought out of the shadows.

There are over 2,350 verses in the Bible that talk about
money and how to deal with money. If we were asked to
sum up all this teaching on money and possessions in one
sentence, it would be this: Don't be a monkey. Just kidding.
It would actually be this: Live an openhanded life. When
you open your hand and give something that's difficult to
deal with over to God, he replaces that empty space in your
palm with peace. So, as you learn to release control of your
money to God, he will replace your financial stress with
financial peace.

Three Truths about Money

There's a constant battle being waged between our desire
to live the type of openhanded life God tells us will be best
for us and our inborn need to hold on to what we can grasp,
desperate to feel in charge of our own security. To help move
us toward God's perspective on money—the perspective that
leads us to freedom—there are three biblical truths we need
to understand:

1. Money Is Personal

We live in a society where we can talk about almost anything. Thanks to social media, we put our lives out there

for the world's consumption without thinking twice. We are willing to share our innermost feelings with friends and total strangers alike. But when the subject of money comes up, the air changes.

Sure, most of us are willing to talk about money in general terms. We discuss who has a lot, who doesn't, taxes, stocks, the economy, and the latest get-rich-quick scheme. But when the subject turns toward our own personal finances, we go quiet. Money feels like a private matter. Why? Because in our society, we are largely defined by how much we make. We equate our self-worth with our net worth. Not only that but talking about our own money can expose deeply held attitudes about consumption or aspects of our personalities that we don't want to put out there for public view.

Given Jesus's assertion that our heart is directly linked to our money, it makes sense that the subject feels so personal. When we expose our income or our own attitudes about money, we are exposing pieces of our heart. We are giving people a glimpse into what's going on deep inside us.

2. Money Is Powerful

That's an understatement, isn't it? Money is one of the most influential entities we interact with throughout the course of our lives. Power can be defined as the ability to modify how others behave. Given that definition, we can all agree that money is powerful. Does it have the ability to modify how we act? More than anything else!

For better or worse, the need for money is what gets most people out of bed in the morning. It determines what clothes they put on, what car they get into, where they go, and what they spend the majority of the day doing. That's pretty powerful, isn't it? Most people spend a large portion of their brain power thinking about money—whether they have enough, how they can get more, what to do about all that they owe.

If you aren't convinced already, consider this question: If you won the lottery today, what would you do tomorrow? Would you get up at the same time? Would you go to work at your current job? Would you keep living in your current house? Would you interact with people in the same way you do today, or would you have more time, ability, and margin to give and love freely? If winning the lottery would change your life drastically (and really, whose life wouldn't it change?), then you can agree that money plays a powerful part in directing the course of your days. It holds power over all of us, whether we like it or not—and as long as we live on this earth, it always will.

3. Money Is Potential

As personal and powerful as money is, when we really step back and look at it, money is nothing more than green ink on a piece of paper, right? In and of itself, it is value neutral—neither inherently good nor bad. Money doesn't spend itself. It takes on the characteristics of the one who is spending it. How you spend the money you have determines whether that money is a positive or a negative force in your life, in your community, and in the world.

There's a common misconception floating around that the Bible says, "Money is the root of all evil." Let us set that straight here and now. The Bible never says money is the root of anything. In an ancient letter to a young pastor named Timothy, the apostle Paul wrote,

> For *the love of money* is the root of all kinds of evil. And some people, craving money, have wandered from the true faith and pierced themselves with many sorrows. (1 Tim. 6:10, emphasis added)

Money is not evil. But the love of money can lead to all kinds of evil. In other words, when our perspective and our priorities get out of order—when we begin to close our fist, putting more trust in money than we do in God—the downward spiral begins. This wraps right back around to the heart issue. Money is tied so completely to the heart of the holder that when it is viewed and used in a way that honors God, it is a powerful tool for life on this earth; but when we make money our top priority, we find ourselves in financial, personal, and relational trouble. Like the monkey who won't open his hand from around his little treasure, we find ourselves caught in the trap of selfishness and crippling materialism.

Materialism is simply a condition in which your heart is more preoccupied with material things than with spiritual things. It isn't a money issue or a possessions issue—it's a heart issue. Debt is a heart issue. Out-of-control spending is a heart issue. Credit card abuse is a heart issue. As we move forward through these pages, we will talk a lot about getting out of debt and getting on a good track financially, but none of the practical steps for getting your financial life straight will amount to anything if you don't first deal with the heart issue. Nothing will change until you commit to letting God's desires for your money and for your life take precedence over your own desires.

You don't have to give up all your money or possessions to avoid materialism or to be in right standing with God. Not by any means. The issue is not how much or how little you have but the condition of your heart. Only one thing can be in control of your life—money or God. As Jesus himself said,

> No one can serve two masters. For you will hate one and love the other; you will be devoted to one and despise the other. You cannot serve God and be enslaved to money. (Matt. 6:24)

Who is in control of your heart right now? Who or what has priority? Are you keeping your fist clamped over what's in your coconut shell? Or are you willing to open your hand and let God replace all your desperate grasping with his peace? The first step is coming to the realization that he owns everything you have anyway. Don't believe us? Read on.

CHAPTER 3

Owner versus Manager

Which One Are You?

GENEROSITY SECRET

Your money is not really your money.

Tell them to use their money to do good. They should be rich in good works and generous to those in need, always being ready to share with others. By doing this they will be storing up their treasure as a good foundation for the future so that they may experience true life.

1 Timothy 6:18–19

Have you ever sat up all night on Christmas Eve or the night before a big birthday and put together one of those "assembly-required" toys for a child? Do you remember the feeling of being so excited to give your child the thing they had been dreaming of . . . the one thing

49

they wanted more than anything else? Maybe you had to go all over town to even find the thing and pay more than you really wanted to, but you did it because you wanted to give your child the desires of their heart.

When my son was younger, I (Nelson) had this experience with him. He had a birthday coming up, and there was one specific toy that he wanted more than he had ever wanted anything in his life. You know how that goes. The only problem was that the toy was new and incredibly popular, which meant it was in short supply.

During my lunch break on the afternoon before his birthday, I set out on a mission to find the one gift that would make my son the (self-proclaimed) happiest little boy in the world. After running in and out of stores all over town, I finally found exactly what I was looking for. The only problem was that it cost close to twice as much as I had expected. But what did I do? Yep, like any good father, I bought my son the toy.

I didn't even realize the thing needed assembly until I got home late that evening. So, after the almost–birthday boy was tucked into bed, I sat up half the night screwing together chunks of plastic. When I was finished, I left the prized possession sitting in the middle of the living room floor so it would be the first thing my son saw on his birthday.

Needless to say, the next morning, he was ecstatic. I have never seen so much jumping up and down and squealing with delight. His attention was glued to this toy that represented so much of my time, effort, and treasure. I was happy that I had been able to give him a good gift. His joy was all the gratitude I needed.

Well, as happens more often than I'd like to admit, watching him play brought out the kid in me. (Can you relate?) I decided I wanted to try the new toy out for myself.

I asked my son, "Hey, can I see that for just a minute?" Any idea what his response was? You got it. In typical little-boy fashion, he replied, "No, Daddy. It's mine." There it is again—that selfish nature. It's easier to see in children because they haven't yet been trained to cover it up in the way we adults have.

Now, I have to admit, my first thought was, *I bought you that toy, and I sat up half the night putting it together. Not to mention I'm a lot bigger than you are. I could reach down and take it away right now . . . or I could go buy you ten more if I decided to. And you are going to tell me no? That it is yours?* Of course, I didn't say any of those things.

But as I sat there watching my son zoom around the living room with his new treasure, I couldn't help but think about how often I have treated God the same way my child had just treated me. How often have I taken the resources and gifts God has given me and set about using them for my own purposes and enjoyment, with little regard for his ultimate ownership? How often have you?

Loosening Your Grip

Giving is not something that comes naturally for us. We like to have total control over our resources. After all, they are ours. We are the ones who got up and went to work for them. They sit in our bank account. We have a right to hold on to them as tightly as we'd like and to do with them as we please. Right? Not exactly.

Just as I paid for and gave my son his new toy, God gives us all the financial resources that come into our lives. James, the brother of Jesus, told us this:

> Whatever is good and perfect is a gift coming down to us from God our Father, who created all the lights in the heavens. (James 1:17)

Everything good in our lives comes from God. The apostle Paul echoed James's words and took things a little further:

> Teach those who are rich in this world not to be proud and not to trust in their money, which is so unreliable. Their trust should be in God, who richly gives us all we need for our enjoyment. (1 Tim. 6:17)

Notice the declaration that God gives us *all we need*. You may have worked hard for the money that has come into your life, but God has given you the breath, health, strength, and intelligence to do your job. He has given you every ounce of the ability to earn your living just as surely as I set that toy on the living room floor for my son to find. As self-made and self-sufficient as you may feel, you are not your own creation.

Notice also that the verse goes on to mention that God richly gives us all we need *for our enjoyment*. God wants us to live blessed lives. He wants us to take pleasure in our days. To be clear, there is absolutely nothing wrong with enjoying the fruits of our labor. We have a responsibility to provide comfortably for our families and to save for the future. God simply wants us to use our money wisely so we have the opportunity to live well and do good for others. Paul went on to say this:

> Tell them to use their money to do good. They should be rich in good works and generous to those in need, always being ready to share with others. By doing this they will be storing up their treasure as a good foundation for the future so that they may experience true life. (1 Tim. 6:18–19)

The problem comes when we fail to recognize where our money and our "toys" come from, when we begin to think we are responsible for all we have and begin to hoard it all for our own pleasure. The solution is the grace-driven paradigm shift we've already been discussing.

If my son had realized that, since I was the source of the money used to buy his birthday gift, it ultimately belonged to me, then he would have been much more willing to share. But just as he did that day, we often live under the false impression that we are the master of whatever finds its way into our hand. Eager not to let a good thing get away, we close our fist around it with no regard for the ultimate source. The only hope we have for letting go of our death grip on our goods is to acknowledge the reality that everything we have belongs to God. He provided it, and it ultimately belongs to him.

> Everything we have belongs to God. He provided it, and it ultimately belongs to him.

All of our money, houses, toys, mutual funds, clothes, gadgets, stocks, and retirement plans are not really our own; they are God's. We've just been entrusted with managing the resources he has allowed into our lives.

Whether we are overseeing huge portfolios or shoestring weekly budgets, we are all managers of God's means. That's actually where the term *stewardship* comes from.

A steward is someone who manages the wealth and property of another. Stewards don't take ownership of their masters' possessions; they don't use them for their own gain. They don't stash a little of the crop away to increase their family's lifestyle. Instead, they distribute their masters' resources as they should be distributed. Part of that means releasing a significant portion of the treasure back into their masters' work.

Part of the paradigm shift to understanding God's ultimate ownership means that we also recognize our role as conduits of his resources. We were not put on earth to amass treasures for ourselves but to let treasure pass through us and back to a greater purpose. The *get all we can while we can* mindset most of us live with is what has driven our culture's financial health off a cliff. In our ignorance, we have turned our perspective away from God and placed it on earthly things that will pass away.

Whether we like to admit it or not, most of us have the impression that the most important thing we can do on this earth is accumulate wealth. But by clutching our material possessions as we constantly search for more, we are fighting a battle we've already lost. We are like the monkey with his hand stuck in the coconut. When Steve Jobs died, he left all his wealth behind—and so will you. Not only that, but you will be held accountable for what you did with it while you were here.

Paul reminds us in Romans 14:12 that one day "each of us will give a personal account to God." In 2 Corinthians 5:10, he reiterates, "For we must all stand before Christ to be judged. We will each receive whatever we deserve for the good or evil we have done in this earthly body." That goes as much for how we handled our money as anything else. Perhaps more so, especially given Jesus's affirmation in Matthew 6:21: "Wherever your treasure is, there the desires of your heart will also be."

God will examine where you laid up your treasure while you were on this earth, and you will have to give an account. In his great work on this subject, *Money, Possessions, and Eternity*, Randy Alcorn writes, "One day everyone must answer these three questions: Where did it all go? What did I spend it on? What has been accomplished for eternity through my use of all this wealth?"[1]

And make no mistake, if you are reading this book, it's a safe bet that you are wealthy. You may not feel like you manage a fortune, but if you are fortunate enough to have warm clothes, a roof over your head, and enough food to eat, you are extremely affluent in the scheme of things.

Alcorn goes on to illustrate this: "Take for example a man or woman who works from age twenty-five to sixty-five and makes 'only' $25,000 a year. . . . This person of modest income (by our standards) will receive a million dollars. He or she will manage a fortune."[2] How will he or she manage it? How will you? Where does it all go? What do you spend it on? What is being accomplished for eternity through your use of all this wealth?

Three Servants and Four Principles

As he often did, Jesus used a parable to teach his first-century listeners about their role in managing their resources. One day, with eager listeners gathered around, he told the story of a wealthy businessman leaving on a long trip. The businessman knew he was going to be away for a while, Jesus explained, so he needed to put someone in charge of his business and all of his wealth. Rather than entrusting everything to one person, he decided to divide the responsibility between three of his servants. Here's how Jesus worded it:

> The Kingdom of Heaven can be illustrated by the story of a man going on a long trip. He called together his servants and entrusted his money to them while he was gone. He gave five bags of silver to one, two bags of silver to another, and one bag of silver to the last—dividing it in proportion to their abilities. He then left on his trip. (Matt. 25:14–15)

The money in this story did not belong to the servants among whom it was divided; it belonged to the master. He was the owner. He simply entrusted his three servants to look after it while he was away. This leads to the first principle of a paradigm-shifting view of money:

Principle 1: The Principle of Possession

Everything You Have Belongs to God

In God's eyes, you are the financial manager of the wealth he has given you. You are not the owner. As we've discussed, God gave you the ability to work for everything you have. He gave you the opportunities that put you where you are today. Everything, including your energy, your intellect, and your ability to produce, is on loan from him. You didn't choose where you were born, what parents you got, or how your brain was wired. You didn't bring anything into the world with you on the day you showed up, and you won't take anything with you when you leave.

This foundational principle is key to changing your financial paradigm. Once you truly grasp that God owns it all, that reality completely changes your relationship with money. When you think it all belongs to you, then you believe that having enough depends solely on you. You worry. You stress. You overwork. But when you realize your wealth belongs to God, you stop worrying so much about where it comes from and start trusting God to give you what you need.

What financial area of your life worries you the most? Credit card debt? Paying off your student loans? Saving for retirement? Starting a new business? Or is it just meeting the basic needs of life month to month? Rest assured that God doesn't want you living in a state of worry about your finances. He wants you to trust him and be confident in the fact that it all belongs to him anyway. He will provide you with what you need for the life he has called you to live— which leads to the second principle we can glean from Jesus's parable.

Principle 2: The Principle of Allocation

God Has Loaned You the Money You Have

God has loaned all of us a portion of wealth to manage. Like the servants in the story, we all get different amounts. The key to being a wise manager has little to do with how much we've been given and more to do with how we handle what we've been given. Let's take a look at what each of the three servant managers decided to do with the owner's money.

The servant who received the five bags of silver began to invest the money and earned five more. The servant with two bags of silver also went to work and earned two more. But the servant who received the one bag of silver dug a hole in the ground and hid the master's money. (Matt. 25:16–18)

The first two servants invested the owner's money wisely. They both put the money to work and doubled what they had been given. They understood an important truth: Money is a tool to be used. The third servant had the wrong perspective. Rather than investing and growing what he had received, he went out and hid his portion in the ground, scared that it might get away from him.

How are you putting to use the money God has loaned you? Are you managing it wisely? Do you invest in others? Do you invest in your family's future? Do you invest in the work of God? Or are you trying to keep it all safe in an account somewhere, afraid that if you let it go you'll end up not having enough? Your answers to these questions matter—and one day, you'll answer them for God himself.

Principle 3: The Principle of Accountability

One Day There Will Be an Audit

Like any good owner, God is watching to see how we handle the money he has loaned us. He is watching to see if we waste it, hoard it, use it all selfishly, invest it wisely, give it generously, or grow it for greater good. God gives us the free will to choose what we will do with our wealth, but he wants to make sure we know that we'll be held accountable for those choices.

After a long time their master returned from his trip and called them to give an account of how they had used his money. The servant to whom he had entrusted the five bags of silver came forward with five more and said, "Master, you gave me five bags of silver to invest, and I have earned five more."

The master was full of praise. "Well done, my good and faithful servant. You have been faithful in handling this small amount, so now I will give you many more responsibilities. Let's celebrate together!"

The servant who had received the two bags of silver came forward and said, "Master, you gave me two bags of silver to invest, and I have earned two more."

The master said, "Well done, my good and faithful servant. You have been faithful in handling this small amount, so now I will give you many more responsibilities. Let's celebrate together!" (Matt. 25:19–23)

The first two servants invested wisely, and the owner was happy. He went so far as to say that since they had been faithful in handling the limited amount he had given them, he would give them even greater responsibility. They had proven they could handle it. But the third servant had not done so well.

Then the servant with the one bag of silver came and said, "Master, I knew you were a harsh man, harvesting crops you didn't plant and gathering crops you didn't cultivate. I was afraid I would lose your money, so I hid it in the earth. Look, here is your money back." (Matt. 25:24–25)

Not only did this guy hoard the money, he also played the victim. He blamed his inability to grow what he had been given on his owner's temperament. He got scared and got good at making excuses. We are often prone to doing the same thing, aren't we? We make poor financial choices. We put something on a credit card that we know we can't pay for. We figure out how to buy a home we can't really afford. And when we find ourselves in a bind financially, we blame the system, the government, our bosses, or even God.

The truth is, what we do with the money we have is our responsibility. When we stand before God and give an account for all that passed through our hands, we will not be able to shift the blame for bad decisions to anyone or anything else. Understanding this reality lays the foundation for the fourth and last principle of healthy financial management.

Principle 4: The Principle of Utilization

God Expects You to Use His Money Wisely

God expects us to use what we've been given wisely. Money is a tool intended to be put to its highest and best use. We'll dive deeply into exactly what that looks like in the chapters ahead. In this parable, the first two servants did a good job using the owner's money well. But fear caused the third servant to close his hand around the money he had been given. He acted like a first-century version of that monkey in the jungle with his hand stuck in a coconut.

How about you? Think about how you handle the money in your life. Are you more like the wise servants or the monkey? When you fully realize that God owns it all and that you are a manager, you will be able to breathe a much-needed sigh of relief. The weight of your financial world is not resting solely on your shoulders. It's better than that. You have a great and generous God who is inviting you into a new paradigm of freedom and impact. God's way of handling money doesn't lead to stress; it leads to significance. But it all begins with letting go of your right to ownership. Choose to see yourself instead as a manager—a wise money manager on a mission for meaning.

CHAPTER 4

Just Say No

What Not to Do with Your Money

> GENEROSITY SECRET
> **The most powerful word for financial freedom is NO.**

*If you are untrustworthy about worldly wealth, who will
trust you with the true riches of heaven?*

Luke 16:11

Most financial how-to books focus on telling you
what to do with your money. And while there
will be plenty of that in these pages, we want
to take this early opportunity to make a few suggestions
for what *not* to do with your money. Because, when you get
right down to it, what you don't do with your money is just
as important as what you do with it.

Where is that fifty-dollar bill and paper heart we asked you to put in a prominent place? Wherever it is, take a minute and just look at it. If you can't actually see it at the moment, picture it in your mind's eye. That fifty dollars is representative of all the money you have. It's a visual example of everything in your bank account. Now, what if we told you to take that fifty-dollar bill off your mirror, board, refrigerator—wherever it is—grab a pair of scissors, and cut it into little pieces. You wouldn't want to do that, would you? You would probably call us crazy and toss this book in the trash. Who would cut up a perfectly good fifty-dollar bill? But, in reality, most of us do exactly that far more often than we realize. We just don't see it in the same terms.

- Have you ever spent fifty dollars at a restaurant because you didn't feel like cooking, even though you had perfectly good food at home? Even worse, have you ever had to throw that same perfectly good food away a couple of days later because it went bad?

- Have you ever walked into a clothing store and bought something that was just a little too tight, rationalizing that it would fit when you lost the couple of pounds you planned to lose? Did that piece of clothing hang in your closet untouched for weeks, months, even years?

- Have you ever gotten a fifty-dollar gift card from someone, stuck it in your wallet, and held on to it because you weren't sure what you wanted to spend it on? Six months later, was it still in your wallet because you really wanted to use it on something special, when you had spent fifty dollars of your own money several times over on things you didn't really need?

- Have you ever gotten a letter from someone trying to raise money for a mission trip and decided not to give because you were stretched pretty tight at that moment but then walked into a restaurant and dropped fifty dollars on a meal you could've easily made at home?

We all make unwise decisions with our money at least some of the time. Our emotions, our appetites, and our desires drive us to treat our money in ways we know aren't rational—but we do it anyway, even the most disciplined among us. We essentially pull that fifty-dollar bill down from its perch and cut it up. Other times, we hold it too tightly or put too much stock in its power. Either way, we are prone to view it in a way that is not at all reflective of how God views our money.

Before we dig into how to get out of debt and find financial freedom, let's look at four things not to do with money.

1. Don't Waste Your Money

New York City is an expensive place to live. Even more so, it's an expensive place to eat. In the decade plus that my (Jennifer's) husband, Brian, and I lived in the city, we spent more than our fair share of money dining out at all the incredible restaurants New York has to offer. In our defense, we were a DINK (Double Income No Kids) couple and foodies to boot. We both love to eat and eat well, so dropping us in the middle of such a food mecca with disposable income was a recipe for, well, wasted money.

Of course, we didn't think of it that way at the time. We were just living our urban, twenty/thirtysomething lives, enjoying all the flavors and offerings of what was around us. But in Manhattan, brunch can easily cost two people sixty dollars or more. And dinner—well, you can imagine. In hindsight, we should've made a few more egg sandwiches in our apartment and put some of that money to better use.

Was there anything wrong with the two of us eating out so much in our early years of marriage? Not necessarily. Was it the wisest use of the money God had entrusted to us? Not necessarily. And apparently we aren't the only ones guilty of overspending in this area. In a recent survey from Charles Schwab, 55 percent of respondents regretted spending money on meals instead of putting that money into a retirement account. According to the survey,

> If, instead of spending so much on eating out, you put $3,000 annually into a 401(k) from age 30 to age 65 and earned a 7% annual return, you'd end up with a nest egg of $414,710— just by redirecting your dining out budget. And, that's a conservative estimate for how much you could save over time, since eating out expenses have been shown to increase by a few hundred dollars every year.[1]

Dining out was the biggest regret cited, but it wasn't the only way people regretted wasting money. Thirty-one percent regretted spending money on expensive clothes or clothes they didn't really need. Twenty-eight percent said they regretted spending so much on cars or vacations. Twenty-six percent wished they hadn't spent so much keeping up with the latest technologies.[2] Let us be clear: there isn't anything inherently wrong with enjoying a nice meal, buying good clothes, or going on vacation, but on the priority list of how you spend your money, none of those things should take the first spot.

Again, we are managers of our money, not owners. When we internalize that fact, we will be more careful about wasting the owner's money on frivolous things. Money is a tool for good, not something to be consumed freely with such little regard for the benefit it could otherwise have—for us, for those around us, and for the world at large.

2. Don't Love Your Money

There's a great line in a popular romantic comedy that says, "The person whose calls you always take . . . that's the relationship you're in." Are you in a love relationship with your money? Do you always take money's calls? In other words, are you always focused on your money—how much you have, how much you need, and how to get more? Do you lie awake at night thinking about money? Do you think if you had more, your life would be better? If you answered yes to any of these questions, you may be in a love relationship with your money.

What you love most will always take top priority in your life. When you allow money to fill that spot, it's no longer available for God and his purposes for your life. As we saw earlier, money is not the root of all evil; the love of money is the root of all evil (1 Tim. 6:10). If we give our allegiance to money, we are no longer focused on the things of God. Remember, Jesus himself said this:

> No one can serve two masters. For you will hate one and love the other; you will be devoted to one and despise the other. You cannot serve God and be enslaved to money. (Matt. 6:24)

Notice Jesus didn't say you should not serve God and money. He says you *cannot*. It's impossible. You have to decide what's going to be the master of your life. What's going to take the place of priority? If anything but God is in that place, everything else will be out of place. The most important decision you can make in life is to put God first in every area—and that includes your money.

3. Don't Trust Your Money

One of the most common mistakes we see people make when it comes to both their financial life and their spiritual life is to put their trust in their money. Too often, money equals security. People set financial security up as their foundation, build on it, and continually work to maintain it. The problem is that finances are not trustworthy. They can sway and shift, which ultimately makes for a weak foundation. As the ancient Proverb says,

> Trust in your money and down you go! (Prov. 11:28)

Jesus once told a story about two different types of people— one who is constantly batted around by the circumstances of life and another who is always able to stand, no matter what the circumstances may be:

> Anyone who listens to my teaching and follows it is wise, like a person who builds a house on solid rock. Though the rain comes in torrents and the floodwaters rise and the winds beat against that house, it won't collapse because it is built on bedrock. But anyone who hears my teaching and doesn't obey it is foolish, like a person who builds a house on sand. When the rains and floods come and the winds beat against that house, it will collapse with a mighty crash. (Matt. 7:24–27)

When your foundation is built on your bank account, your stocks, or your retirement plan, what do you do when those things begin to wane? And, trust us, at some point they will wane, no matter how good a money manager you are. Worldly wealth is fickle and fleeting. If you lose your job, the market tanks, or there's a major medical event in your family, things can change in an instant. Financial security is like the shifting sand. When the storms of life beat against it, it can "collapse with a mighty crash."

Instead of putting your faith and security in your money, if you have been prone to doing that, consider putting it in a more reliable place—in God and his Son, Jesus. If you are already a follower of Jesus, you know that he is your source. Take a minute to step back and examine whether you have been trusting in him for your security and well-being or whether you have been trusting in money and your own ability to produce. If you have fallen into the common trap of putting faith in your finances over faith in God, take a few minutes now and repent of that. Simply tell God you are sorry for trusting in your money. Invite him back in to be the Lord over your entire life, including your financial life.

If you aren't a Christian, you may be a little uncomfortable with where this is going. But these truths are foundational to changing your financial paradigm—really your life paradigm—and allowing you to step out of stress and into a life of freedom and peace. The only foundation worth building your life on is the foundation of God. Jesus himself said this:

> I am the way, the truth, and the life. No one can come to the Father except through me. (John 14:6)

Later, he asks his own disciples—people who had walked with him for years, seen him perform miracles, and listened to his teaching and his claims—this question:

> Who do you say I am? (Mark 8:29)

Eventually, we all have to answer the same question, don't we? We all have to make a decision about who we believe Jesus is. There are really only two possible answers. Either we embrace who Jesus says he is, or we reject his teaching totally and continue on our way. There is no middle ground. Take a look at how C. S. Lewis, one of the most influential writers and apologists for the Christian faith, once posited the options:

> I am trying here to prevent anyone saying the really foolish thing that people often say about Him: "I'm ready to accept

Jesus as a great moral teacher, but I don't accept His claim to be God." That is the one thing we must not say. A man who was merely a man and said the sort of things Jesus said would not be a great moral teacher, He would either be a lunatic—on a level with the man who says he is a poached egg—or else would be the Devil of Hell. You must make your choice. Either this man was, and is, the Son of God; or else a madman or something worse. You can shut Him up for a fool; you can spit at Him and kill Him as a demon; or you can fall at His feet and call Him Lord and God. But let us not come with any patronizing nonsense about His being a great moral teacher. He has not left that open to us. He did not intend to.[3]

When we acknowledge Jesus as the Son of God and accept the free gift of salvation that God has offered through him (John 3:16), we gain forgiveness for our sins, a relationship with the One who created us, and eternity in heaven. If you are ready to invite Jesus into your life or if you'd like some more detail on what that really means, turn to chapter 15 or go to www.TheGenerositySecret.com.

With God and his Son as the foundation for your life— rather than your finances, your relationships, your health, or any other thing—you can face any and all difficulties that come your way with faith and peace. He is the only One worthy of placing your trust in. And as you do, he will begin to shift the paradigm that determines your worldview from the inside out. Slowly but surely, you will begin to see your money as a tool for God's purposes, your stress will dissipate, and you will be able to walk not only in the overall freedom that comes through knowing Jesus but also in complete financial freedom.

4. Don't Expect Your Money to Satisfy

Benjamin Franklin has been quoted as saying, "Money has never made man happy, nor will it. There is nothing in its nature to produce happiness. The more of it one has the more one wants." You may have heard the anecdotal story that bears this truth: A financial planner walked into a room of people who had come to hear him speak and asked the question, "How much money do you think you would need to earn to be able to live comfortably and alleviate financial stress from your life?"

The answers were interesting. People in the room who made $40,000 said that $50,000 would put them where they wanted to be. People who made $50,000 claimed that $65,000 would be the magic number for them. Those who made $65,000 to $70,000 said that $90,000 a year would solve all of their financial troubles. The overwhelming answer was essentially, "I need $10,000 to $20,000 more per year, and *then* I'll be happy / be able to get out of debt / be able to live the lifestyle I want to live."

No matter how much money you have, human nature is to think you don't have quite enough. You need just a little more and then you'll be okay, right? This is a fallacy we all buy into when we expect money to satisfy. If you think more money will allow you to have all you need, you are expecting too much from your money. You are asking it to provide security and contentment that it is not capable of providing. If you think having more will make you happier, more secure, more important, more valuable, or more fulfilled, you will end up disappointed every time. You will always find that when you get to the financial level at which you thought everything would fall into place, the needle will move, and you'll think you need a little more.

In the next section, we will examine the idea of contentment; that is, the truth that money is not capable of satisfying and what you can do in light of that truth. For now, take a look at this excerpt from a letter the apostle Paul wrote to early believers in the city of Philippi in the eastern part of modern-day Greece.

> If you think more money will allow you to have all you need, you are expecting too much from your money.

> I know how to live on almost nothing or with everything. I have learned the secret of living in every situation, whether it is with a full stomach or empty, with plenty or little. For I can do everything through Christ, who gives me strength. (Phil. 4:12–13)

When you expect money to satisfy, you will always be chasing, searching, grasping for more. You will be running after an illusion of contentment that doesn't exist. Doesn't that sound exhausting? Thankfully, there is a better way to live.

A Better Way

Back to that fifty-dollar bill. You may consider fifty dollars a lot of money, or you may think it's an insignificant amount. No matter where you fall on the spectrum, think again of that fifty dollars as representing everything in your bank account, everything in your retirement account, all of your investments, and all of your stuff.

- Would you want to take scissors and cut it up until it's worthless? Of course not.
- Would you sleep with it in your bed and profess your love for it? That sounds pretty ridiculous, doesn't it?
- Would you trust it to support and hold you through difficult times? Probably not.
- Would you expect it to satisfy your deepest longings, bringing you peace and contentment? For all its promises, we feel sure that you know it can't do that.

When you look at it in those simple terms, it's easy to see that you shouldn't waste your money, love your money, trust your money, or expect your money to satisfy. Instead, allow yourself to begin seeing money as a tool for greater good—a means to a happier end, if you will. Choose to let your paradigm shift, acknowledging that God is the owner of all you have and you are simply the manager. Open your hand and let go of the treasure that is controlling your life. Then and only then will you find peace and true prosperity. Time to dive into the details for getting there.

Part 2

Breaking Free from Debt for Good

Opening Your Hand

How Generosity Is the First Step in Becoming Debt-Free

GENEROSITY SECRET
Learning to give leads to financial freedom.

Since you excel in so many ways—in your faith, your gifted speakers, your knowledge, your enthusiasm, and your love from us—I want you to excel also in this gracious act of giving.

2 Corinthians 8:7

An inclination to give is written on your soul, no matter how muted it may be by your innate bent toward self-preservation, present concerns, or lack of belief. Sometimes it takes a traumatic experience to bring that God-given pull toward generosity to the surface. Horror novelist

Stephen King is not someone who is usually associated with sharing timeless biblical principles. But in a commencement speech delivered to Vassar graduates, he offered some powerful insights to his audience on living an openhanded life. Here's an excerpt of his comments:

> All the money you earn, all the stocks you buy, all the mutual funds you trade—all of that is mostly smoke and mirrors. It's still going to be a quarter-past getting late whether you tell the time on a Timex or a Rolex. No matter how large your bank account, no matter how many credit cards you have, sooner or later things will begin to go wrong with the only three things you have that you can really call your own: your body, your spirit and your mind.
>
> So I want you to consider making your life one long gift to others. And why not? All you have is on loan, anyway. All that lasts is what you pass on. . . .
>
> We have the power to help, the power to change. And why should we refuse? Because we're going to take it with us? Please. Giving is a way of taking the focus off the money we make and putting it back where it belongs—on the lives we lead, the families we raise, the communities that nurture us.
>
> So I ask you to begin giving, and to continue as you began. I think you'll find in the end that you got far more than you ever had, and did more good than you ever dreamed.[1]

Who knows how familiar Mr. King is with the Old Testament. We wouldn't venture a guess. But intentionally or otherwise, his remarks on giving perfectly support the observation in the book of Ecclesiastes that "we all come to the end of our lives as naked and empty-handed as on the day we were born. We can't take our riches with us" (Eccles.

5:15). They also echo the mindset that takes the sting out of this condition, as spoken by Jesus in the New Testament: "It is more blessed to give than to receive" (Acts 20:35). Anyone who has much experience with giving knows this to be true.

The Surprising Thing about Generosity

In his famous letter to the believers in Corinth, Paul wrote,

> Since you excel in so many ways—in your faith, your gifted speakers, your knowledge, your enthusiasm, and your love from us—I want you to excel also in this gracious act of giving. (2 Cor. 8:7)

Paul's words may strike you as a little confusing. First of all, why would he say "gracious act of giving"? Second, what does it even look like to excel in giving?

As we've already established, letting go of money we've earned is not always easy. If we aren't living under the right paradigm, we won't want to let go of what has been given to us. We have a natural instinct to keep our fist tightly closed over the treasure in our hand. So giving in the way God wants us to give requires grace—grace he provides as we begin to trust his ultimate control over our financial life. We need God's grace as we begin giving and as we walk along the path toward becoming more generous givers.

Now, let's think about this business of excelling in giving. How can you excel in giving? Paul simply means that you become excellent at being a giver. How? First and foremost, by recognizing that giving is the path to peace with money.

The way you become financially healthy is by paying attention to your God-given inclination to give and then choosing to engage in the adventure.

But maybe you're not there yet. Most of us have to learn to excel in this gracious act of giving by taking small steps. If you think about it, everything you have ever excelled at in life happened in stages. You can't go from zero to sixty without learning how to shift the gears in between.

This reality hit me (Nelson) one night—quite a while before the birthday surprise incident—as I was walking with my then two-and-a-half-year-old son through a park. (It's amazing all the things that being a parent will teach you.) He was stomping in mud puddles and doing all the things two-and-a-half-year-olds do when it dawned on me that he had really mastered this thing called walking. Now, that may not sound too impressive, but it hadn't been very long at all since he'd entered what I like to call step one of the learning-to-excel-at-walking process.

Step one started when he was about six months old. One day, he taught himself how to project his body forward in some identifiable way. He would lie on his stomach and put his elbows out and scoot forward like an inchworm. I called it the army crawl. He couldn't stand up or walk yet, but he was getting started.

Then, a little while later, he began step two. Out of the blue, he figured out how to make his arms and legs work together so that he could crawl. And once he learned to crawl, man could he crawl! He zoomed around so fast I couldn't keep up with him.

Obviously, as time passed, he had to advance past the crawling stage. He couldn't crawl around on his hands and knees forever. So he moved on to step three, which I like to call the wobbly-baby phase. He learned to pull himself up and hold on to something to walk himself from one place to the next. He would be leaning on the couch and then somehow make his way over to the chair, using something solid to support himself as he went.

Then, all of a sudden, one day he was walking with confidence. Now he has mastered simple walking, and he's moved on to running, jogging, and skipping. He has learned to excel at this new skill by going through a series of steps.

If you are going to learn to excel at anything in life—whether it's driving a car, learning a foreign language, or perfecting a golf swing—you have to progress through a series of steps or stages. The same holds true for learning to honor God with your finances.

Now, as part of getting on the right track toward financial freedom, it's important that we do a number of things:

- Get out of debt.
- Live within our means..
- Break the bonds of materialism.
- Make wise financial decisions.

While we will explore all of these things in detail, none of them will get us where we want to go if we haven't first discovered and embraced the power of the Generosity Secret. Again, generosity is the secret. Learning to give leads to financial freedom.

We know you may not believe us yet, but it's true: the first step in getting out of debt and moving toward financial freedom is becoming generous. The key to breaking the bonds of materialism and making wise financial decisions is giving in a God-honoring way. And learning to live within your means takes on a whole new significance when your means become infused by God's blessing on your generosity. The way we ultimately honor God and begin cooperating with him in our financial lives is through our giving. We learn to excel, or to become excellent, at giving. How can you excel at giving in a God-honoring way? It all starts with giving an initial gift back to God.

How to Take the First Step

Learning to live a life of generosity begins by deciding to give an initial gift back to God. There is nothing grand or complicated about it. Acting out of your new paradigm, acknowledging that your financial resources are actually God's and that you are just the manager, you decide to give a gift back to him. That gift gets you started on the path of generosity. Now, let us say upfront, this isn't a good place to stay, but it's a good place to start.

Giving for the first time can be scary. Even though you want to begin honoring God by giving back to him, you will inevitably have questions and doubts. What if you give and then you are strained financially? What if you can't make ends meet as it is? How will the money you give be spent? These are all questions that keep people from taking steps toward a life of financial freedom and peace. They are valid concerns that all new givers struggle with.

This kind of struggle is part of the human condition. Day after day we find ourselves in situations that put our heads and our hearts in conflict with each other. Even when we know what we should do, as in the case of giving, the fear of actually doing it sometimes paralyzes us.

The apostle Paul understood our struggle well. He admitted to facing it in his own life:

> I have discovered this principle of life—that when I want to do what is right, I inevitably do what is wrong. I love God's law with all my heart. But there is another power within me that is at war with my mind. This power makes me a slave to the sin that is still within me. Oh, what a miserable person I am! (Rom. 7:21–24)

As long as we are walking this earth, we will be caught in a war that pits our faith in Jesus's ways against the "common-sense" leanings of our nature. Many of this war's confrontations are played out on the battlefield of giving.

Fear is one of the primary enemies of heartfelt generosity. Fear keeps people locked in the lie of the scarcity mentality—the idea that the more I give away, the less I will have for my own needs. The only way to break out of that lie is to take the first step in faith. Decide on an amount and give it. This will put you squarely on the path toward experiencing God's best for your financial life. We love what the founder of the modern Christian missions movement, William Carey, had to say on the subject:

> I was once young and now I am old, but not once have I been witness to God's failure to supply my need when first I had given for the furtherance of His work. He has never failed in His promise, so I cannot fail in my service to Him.[2]

As much as Paul understood the struggle we have with ourselves, he also knew that following God's commands and principles was not something that should be determined by our feelings. Sometimes we just have to decide to get started with what's right, no matter how we may feel about it at the time. Emotions are fleeting, but God's truth about his plan for our financial lives is timeless. In a letter to Christians in Corinth, Paul wrote:

> Now about the collection for the Lord's people. . . . On the first day of every week, each one of you should set aside a sum of money in keeping with your income. (1 Cor. 16:1–2 NIV)

In this passage, Paul gives us some detail on how we ought to bring our gift back to God. First of all, he talks about how much we are supposed to give—a sum in keeping with our income. The Bible never tells us to give a specific dollar amount. Never do we hear, "To honor God, you must give one hundred dollars every week." Of course not. The issue isn't a dollar amount but rather how proportionate our gift is to our income.

Ultimately, giving is about our level of sacrifice. If you make just a little bit of money, you are expected to give only a little bit. If you don't make anything, you aren't expected to give anything. Your giving should be directly, proportionally tied to what God allows to come into your life. The amount should be enough to prove that your hand isn't closed over what you have.

College students always have a lot of questions on this issue. Many of them want to give but don't have an income while they are in school. They'll approach us and say, "I want to give, but I don't know how much I should give since I don't have any real income coming in . . ." We always tell them that, biblically, they don't have to give yet. People with no income aren't expected to give. Still, we encourage them to give a little when they can, just to get started on the right financial path and begin establishing a habit for when they are blessed with an income, no matter how large or small.

By choosing to give a gift back to God, you are essentially saying, "God, I am thankful for the life, health, breath, oxygen, and intelligence you have given me to be able to earn this money. Apart from you, I wouldn't have anything in my life. So I am going to honor you by returning to you part of what you've given me." When you do this, you invite God to be part of your finances. And wouldn't you rather give to God and have his blessing on your money than block him from becoming involved in your financial life? We contend that the fear of operating apart from God is worse than the fear of running short on money if you give.

When to Give

Back to the details of giving an initial gift, Paul also tells us when we should give—on the first day of every week. This assertion gives us a great opportunity to build a bridge of application from the ancient context of Paul's writing to our modern-day lives. In biblical times, everybody got paid on the last day of the week. So they brought part of that income to the temple on the first day of the week. Pretty simple.

Things don't work out quite so easily in our day. Some people still get paid at the end of the week, while others get paid every two weeks or once a month or once a year or when they close a big deal or when they land a gig. You get the picture. In our modern culture, people's pay schedules are all over the place.

So how can we apply Paul's instruction to bring our gift on the first day of every week? Look at the timeless principle in Paul's instruction: *Return a gift to God when you get paid.* It's as simple as that. Set up a system that allows you to give back to God when you get paid. Put him in line ahead of the bills and the Mexican restaurant. Let his gift be the very first money that comes out of your paycheck.

Not only that, but as the Corinthians did, we should return our gift in a way that is both identifiable and accountable.

Make Your Gift Count

When you decide to step out of financial stress and begin pursuing financial freedom, make sure you give your initial gift in a way that is identifiable and by which you can be held accountable. That means, first of all, that when you give your gift to your local church, do it through whatever offering system they have in place. If your church provides offering envelopes, make sure you give using an offering envelope. Or maybe you can give to your church online or through an app. Just make sure you do it in a way that will ensure that the church leaders know you gave.

People sometimes question this by bringing up Jesus's words:

Watch out! Don't do your good deeds publicly, to be admired by others, for you will lose the reward from your Father in

> heaven. . . . Give your gifts in private, and your Father, who
> sees everything, will reward you. (Matt. 6:1, 4)

Many people think that this passage means they should give without any kind of acknowledgment. But that's an incorrect interpretation. In reality, it means that you shouldn't tell other people the amount you are giving. You shouldn't brag about the fact that you give or disclose the dollar amount of your gifts to your friends and relatives. In no way does it mean that your church leaders shouldn't know.

Scripture goes on to tell us that those who have been appointed leaders within the church should know what people are giving back to God. In fact, Mark recounts the story of Jesus sitting by the collection box in the temple, watching as people brought their gifts (Mark 12:41). In the book of Acts, givers actually brought their gifts to the church and laid them at the pastor's feet. Aren't you glad we don't have to do that today?

Even though we have moved away from ancient methods of giving to more modern options, the principle remains the same. You must give your gift in a way that is identifiable to your church leaders. Why? So that they will be able to hold you accountable for your giving—not so they can lord it over you, but so they can report back to you on what you've given and how it is being used. And so you have a record of your giving for your taxes.

There's also another, perhaps more important, reason you should give in an identifiable and accountable way. Doing so lets your church leaders know that you have taken a step toward generosity and puts them in a better position to help you along the path toward financial freedom.

The First Step to Becoming Debt-Free

Being able to open your hand and give an initial gift back to God signifies a shift in your financial paradigm. For the first time, you are making a practical acknowledgment that you are not the source of your income, that you are simply the manager of what has been entrusted to you. That adjustment in perspective is foundational to walking away from the bondage of debt and getting started on your new path toward financial freedom.

GENEROSITY SECRET

Giving to God is the first step toward getting out of debt.

It's time to begin putting the truth of the Generosity Secret into practice. It's time to do something with the fifty-dollar bill that has been staring back at you for the last several days or weeks. The first step toward financial transformation is not saving money for your own needs—again, that's the conventional wisdom of a cultural paradigm born of greed. The way to create a lasting glitch in the cycle you are caught in is to take an initial step toward generosity. To give to God, no matter how much debt you are in or what your current financial situation looks like.

Are you ready to take the first step? Now is the time. Open your hand and decide to give that fifty dollars back to God as an acknowledgment that he is the source of all you have, as an acknowledgment that you are simply the manager of the resources he has given you, as an acknowledgment that you are ready to invite him into your financial life. This is where everything begins to change.

Take that fifty-dollar bill off your mirror, refrigerator, or wherever you've had it, and give it back to God's work around you in an identifiable way. (Hold on to the paper heart with your debt-free date on it, and tack it back up where you'll see it regularly.) Go to church and put the fifty dollars in a giving envelope. Or deposit it into your checking account and immediately give online. If you aren't connected with a local church yet, pray about a charity God may want you to support, and give the fifty dollars to it. When you take this step, you are breaking the cycle of financial strain in your life. You are shifting your perspective. You are opening your heart to God's way of money management and inviting his blessing into your financial life. Congratulations. Get ready to watch him work. You are in for an exciting ride.

CHAPTER 6

Down with Debt

The Three Most Important Financial Decisions You Can Make

—— GENEROSITY SECRET ——

Don't spend your money before you have it.

Owe nothing to anyone—except for your obligation to love one another.

Romans 13:8

What would life look like for you if you didn't have any monthly payments? Can you imagine such a reality? How much would you be able to give, save, and spend each month if you didn't have to pay Visa or MasterCard? Take it a step further and imagine not having an auto loan hanging over your head. Getting even more radical, what would it feel like to have your house on a fifteen-year mortgage that you're close to paying off instead of a thirty-year mortgage that you're barely making headway on? What would it feel like to pay your rent without a struggle? You may wonder if living this way in the modern world is even possible. It is—but only when you abandon the world's paradigm for money management and embrace the subversive ways of the One who owns it all.

You may be so steeped in a debt mindset that you don't even realize how bound you are. Let's look at a few signs that you may be stuck in a debt trap.

- **Your debt is growing.** Is the balance on your credit card(s) bigger this month than it was last month? Bigger than it was this time last year? If so, you are likely using credit to maintain a lifestyle your salary can't support.

- **You delay payments or pay only the minimum due.** If the minimum payment is all you can afford to pay when your credit card bill comes in, then you are digging your financial hole deeper with every passing month. You are throwing money away. Think about this: If you have a credit card with a $5,000 balance and you just make the minimum payments, it will take you thirteen years to pay off the debt, and you will have paid an additional $4,000 in interest. You are caught in a trap that is benefiting your captors.

- **You don't feel like you're able to give or save.** If you aren't saving for your future because you can't afford to, you are in a dangerous place. What if God were to ask you to give a sacrificial gift or go on a mission trip? Would you be able to? Or would your debt make that impossible? If debt is holding you back from giving and/or saving, it's time to get out.

- **If you miss a paycheck, you can't pay your bills.** If your paycheck was late this month and that would cause you to be late on your mortgage or other bills, something is wrong. God wants you to have more margin than that in your life.

- **You made at least one impulsive purchase last week.** Think back over the last week. Did you make any unplanned or unneeded purchases? Maybe you bought clothes you didn't need or upgraded your phone when your old one was fine. Impulsive purchases are a sign that you're being unwise with your money.

- **You are constantly worried about money.** Being in debt will cause you stress. It will cause you to lose sleep and even put strain on your relationships. Money problems are cited as the number-one reason for divorce in America.

Here's the countercultural truth: financial health doesn't come from making more money. It comes from making wise, godly decisions with the money you already have. And that begins with getting out of debt. If you keep doing what you've always done, what's popular and accepted, you'll keep getting what you've always gotten—high payments, the inability to save or give, stress, and financial strain. If you want something different, it's going to require making different decisions. Start with these three.

Decision 1: Get Out of Debt

In chapter 1, we asked you to make a bold decision. We asked you to do this:

Decide to get out of debt!

Did you make the debt decision? Did you decide to trade in the prevailing way of operating in the world for a better way? For the path of freedom? If not, now is the time to do just that. Yes, at first it can feel scary to decide to give up on debt, but it is the wisest possible move you can make financially. The best way to build wealth and create financial freedom in your life is to become and stay debt-free. It's one of the not-so-secret secrets of the wealthiest people in America. They live on less than they make and spend only when they have the money in their bank account to spend.

The timeless principles of Scripture support this idea of not carrying debt. In a letter to early believers in Rome, Paul wrote, "Owe nothing to anyone—except for your obligation to love one another" (Rom. 13:8). In the book of Proverbs, King Solomon, a man widely renowned for his wisdom, warned, "The borrower is servant to the lender" (22:7). These are just two admonitions of many. The message is clear: When you live with debt hanging over your head, you are not living your best life. You are handcuffed. You are a slave, as King Solomon said. To break free from the debt norm in our society, you have to intentionally choose to walk another way . . . and not listen to the voices from the crowd that try to pull you back into the debt trap. Their voices will be loud, trust us.

Years ago, there was a study done on—you guessed it—monkeys. A group of monkeys was locked in a room with a pole at the center. Some ripe bananas were put at the top of the pole to beckon the monkeys upward. Whenever a monkey would start to climb the pole, researchers would knock him off with a blast of water from a fire hose. Every single time a monkey tried to climb, he'd be blasted off, until every monkey had been knocked off the pole repeatedly, thus learning that the climb was hopeless.

Here's where it gets more interesting. After some time, the researchers replaced a single monkey with a new one who didn't know the system. As soon as the new monkey started to climb the pole, the other monkeys would pull him down and punish him for trying. One by one, each monkey was replaced and the scene repeated until there were no monkeys left in the room that had been blasted with water. Still, none of them could climb the pole. If one tried, the other monkeys would pull that brave soul down every time. The monkeys had no idea why they behaved this way; they just knew they couldn't get to those bananas.[1]

When you decide to debunk debt and begin the climb toward a different way of living, you'll have some monkeys trying to pull you down. You'll have people telling you that debt is a tool, that you need debt to function in society, that debt is just a necessary part of life. All of these things are untruths that have permeated the culture we live in. Expect to hear these lies spouted loudly and often while you focus your attention and efforts on creating a better way of life for you and your family.

If you want to become debt-free, it begins with a commitment to begin listening to God and his ways regarding your finances. At its core, debt isn't a math issue or even an income issue, though sometimes it may feel that way. Debt is a behavioral issue. It's a heart issue and ultimately a spiritual issue. If your debt is growing, you are living in a way that goes against God's best plan for you. As the psalmist wrote,

> The wicked borrow and never repay;
>   but the godly are generous givers. (Ps. 37:21)

Living in a way that is counter to God's always produces stress. And while God never promised a stress-free life, he doesn't want you to live with the pressure that comes from being upside down in your finances. He offers such a better way. Before you read any further, if you haven't already made the decision to get out of debt, do make it now. Tell God, "I'm tired of living this way. With your help, I commit to becoming debt-free."

Giving the fifty-dollar bill was a powerful first step in your journey to getting out of debt. In so many cases, the decision to become debt-free is a greed-driven decision. Choosing to give first illustrates that your motivation is not simply your own best interests but rather a new commitment to God's way of generosity. Debt is the result of being shackled to greed. Giving at the beginning of this process breaks the bonds of greed and consumerism and signals your commitment to the new paradigm. Giving to God will never slow down your path to financial freedom; it will only accelerate it.

Decision 2: Live on Less than You Make

Living on less than you make sounds like such a simple thing to do, doesn't it? But, in our culture, it's much harder than it sounds. The number-one cause of debt in America is the fact that our yearnings exceed our earnings. We live in a competitive consumer society where keeping up with the family down the street has become an acceptable goal. And we bury ourselves in debt to achieve it. While it's easy to think, *Well, if I made more money, I wouldn't have this problem*, that's just not true. Remember our study about how much money people thought they needed to be happy? It's always just a little more than they already have.

Once you make the decision to get out of debt, the best way to start getting there is to commit to living on less than you make. Consider this comparison:

Couple A makes $57,000 per year and lives on $56,500.
Couple B makes $57,000 per year and lives on $57,500.

Which couple has more peace when it comes to their money? Which couple lives with financial stress that only gets worse and worse over time?

Financial freedom is not found in making more money; it's found in mastering a certain set of principles that apply no matter how much money you have coming in. First, deciding to get out of debt. Second, committing to living on less than you make. After all, the whole reason you are in debt is because you are spending more than you make. Instead of living within your means, you are living on over 100 percent of your income—which just means you keep digging deeper and deeper into debt with every passing month and every passing year.

Living on less than you make isn't possible without a shift in priorities. When your financial priorities are right, you position yourself for God's financial blessing and the margin that is essential to financial freedom. This begins with making sure you are giving to God and saving/investing for your own future before anything else. In chapter 10, we'll explain in detail a principle called the 70 Percent Principle of Lasting Wealth. This principle is the lynchpin for getting your financial house in order. For now, just begin to internalize the idea of learning to live on less than you make. No matter how difficult or scary that may sound, we assure you it's worth the effort.

Decision 3: Add No New Debt

As soon as you make the decision to get out of debt and commit to living on less than you make, you will be tempted to add debt in another area or in a different way. After all, you're still living in a world that screams, "Debt is good! Get what you want now and pay later!" Plus you will still be hardwired with your old habits. So your decision to get out of debt has to be followed up with a commitment to break old habits and to not add anything new to your existing debt.

One way to start breaking the old, ingrained way of thinking is to start using cash to pay for things. Do you think that sounds old school? Maybe so, but in the old school most people weren't drowning in credit card payments. Studies show that if you walk into a store with a credit card (even a debit card), you will spend 23 percent more than if you walk in with cash. It's easier to buy now when all you have to do is swipe, and especially when you don't really have to pay until later. You don't even feel like you are spending real money.

What if, for a time, you committed to using cash to pay for the things you need? Go to the bank at the beginning of the week, take out enough cash to pay for what you need that week, and commit to not swiping or typing in your credit card number a single time. Decide that if you can't pay cash for something, you're not going to buy it.

Let's have a little more fun with paper and scissors. Add up how many credit cards you have—don't leave any of them out. Now print or write out the following verse:

Be satisfied with what you have. (Heb. 13:5)

Make as many copies of this verse as the cards you have, cut the verses out, and tape one to the back of every single one of your credit cards. You may even want to tape one to the back of your debit cards too. While using your debit cards obviously doesn't lead directly to debt, it still allows you to spend more easily than may be wise. We're not telling you to stop using your debit cards completely, but we do suggest transitioning to cash as much as possible as you get your financial life straightened out. And it wouldn't hurt to have this reminder from Hebrews staring you in the face every time you start to buy something.

The Discipline of Debt-Free Living

We've heard it said that 20 percent of money management is about knowledge and 80 percent is about behavior. If you ever hope to get out of debt and make it all the way to financial freedom, you have to behave yourself into a new way of operating. Again, that begins with adopting God's view concerning money and possessions. It continues with being disciplined enough to make the three decisions we've just explored:

1. Get out of debt.
2. Live on less than you make.
3. Add no new debt.

Next, you have to have the discipline to approach each area of your financial life with a specific game plan built on wisdom and intentionality, which we'll discuss in the next chapter.

The word *discipline* comes from the term *disciple*. A disciple is simply a student or follower of a teacher, leader, or philosopher. The ultimate goal of your financial life is that it will be surrendered to and empowered by God himself. He wants to work in and through you to impact the world around you. Teaching you to open your hand to him financially so that your heart is also open is one of his greatest tools for growing you into the likeness of his Son. Remember, it is impossible to become a fully developing follower of Jesus without also becoming a fully developing steward of your financial resources. That's why this is so important. It's not just about your money.

CHAPTER 7

Get Out and Stay Out

A Practical Plan for Showing Debt the Door

GENEROSITY SECRET

Know the facts about your financial life.

A house is built by wisdom
and becomes strong through good sense.
Proverbs 24:3

To get where you want to go, you have to know where you are. Once you've made the three essential debt decisions discussed in the last chapter, it's time to create a plan for getting out of debt. The first step is to get honest about how your financial picture looks right this minute. Surprisingly, many people have no idea exactly how much debt they are in, what their interest rates are, how much of their monthly income is going toward debt, or even how much income they have coming in. Without clarity on where you stand right now and a clear road map for getting where you want to go, you won't to be able to make a successful journey.

Once you get a firm grasp on your current reality, it's time to set up a plan and take some specific actions to invite God into this process of handling your finances in a way that is honoring to him. Are you ready to get down to business and start kicking debt out the door? Here is your four-step plan for doing just that:

Step 1: Make a List of Your Debts and Assets

To put that in non–financial planner language, make a list of what you owe (debts/liabilities) and what you own (assets). You need to be able to see the actual numbers on a piece of paper. To keep it simple, we'll provide space for you to begin this process right here. (There are also downloadable worksheets available for you at www.TheGenerositySecret.com.) Let's start with your liabilities. How much do you owe in the following areas:

- Credit cards (make sure you include all of them): _____
- Student loans: _____
- Car loans: _____
- Personal loans: _____
- Unpaid bills: _____
- Unpaid taxes: _____
- Other (think alimony, payroll loans, lease agreements, etc.): _____

- Other: _____
  Total: _____

How do you feel when you look at that number? Are you in less debt than you thought you were? More? Does the number scare you? No matter what you have just written on that total line, try not to be intimidated. You just took an important step in your financial journey. Now let's look at your assets:

- Bank account: _____
- Savings: _____
- Stocks: _____
- Retirement funds: _____
- Other investments: _____
- Home: _____
- Property: _____
- Valuables: _____
- Other: _____
- Other: _____
  Total: _____

Having a firm grasp of these numbers is extremely important to beginning the process of becoming debt-free. Only when you see them laid out in black and white can you clearly answer necessary questions, such as these:

- Exactly how much debt are you carrying?
- Do your assets outweigh your liabilities, or do you have a negative net worth?

- Do you need to sell some of your assets to begin paying off your debts?

While these questions can be intimidating, you've just worked through an essential part of getting on the path to financial freedom. Knowing the truth of your situation is a prerequisite to changing it. As Jesus so famously said, "You will know the truth, and the truth will set you free" (John 8:32).

Step 2: Set Up and Begin a Repayment Plan

You will never get out of debt accidentally. You need a plan. So often, we counsel people who think that one day they'll just happen to be in a position to get out of debt. They think their income will go up or they'll get a big bonus or a relative with money will die and leave them an inheritance, and then they'll be able to pay off their debts. This kind of thinking leads only to more debt, more money blown in interest payments, and lots of wasted time.

If you are in debt, now is the time to figure out a plan to start working your way out. As Proverbs 21:5 teaches, "Good planning and hard work lead to prosperity." So, to turn this ship around, it's time to start planning and working your plan. If you can, we suggest meeting with a financial advisor who can help you take stock of your current situation and recommend the best way to begin paying down your debt.

We won't go into detail about budgeting here. There are many great budgeting resources readily available to you. For a list of ones we recommend, go to www.TheGenerositySecret.com. In short, make sure you are budgeting your money. No one likes the idea of budgeting, but it's nonnegotiable if you want to handle your finances wisely.

If you aren't budgeting, chances are you're spending more than you make each month. Think back to the decision you made in the last chapter to live on less than you make. The only way to ensure you do that is to create a budget that details how much you make versus every dollar that comes out of that amount during the month. If you aren't able to cover all your expenses with some margin left given your current income and outflow, start looking for areas where you can cut back. Here are a few suggestions:

- Lower your cable bill or quit cable altogether.
- Call your wireless carrier and inquire about a less-expensive plan.
- Drop movie- and television-streaming services.
- Find a cheaper gym.
- Eat more meals at home.
- Make your own coffee and skip the coffee shop.
- Use slightly older technology.
- Pause before you buy new clothes.

Your income will be your greatest tool to get you out of debt. But it can't do that for you if you are spending every dollar you make and then some. Get serious about cutting expenses and creating some margin in your month.

Once you've taken a hard look at your budget and how it is working or not working in your favor, it's time to create a debt-repayment plan. Our personal favorite is the debt-snowball method of repayment. To begin working the debt snowball, list all your debts in order of the smallest payoff balance to the largest payoff balance. This includes every debt you listed on your liability sheet above and should be everything you owe outside of your home mortgage. List everything in order of smallest to largest debt, without regard for interest rates.

Once you've listed your debts, work to pay off the smallest one first while you continue to pay the minimum payment to stay current on all the others. Get serious about paying off that smallest debt. Every extra dollar you can find in your budget should go toward it. If you can sell something and put that money toward the payment, that's great. Do what you have to do to pay it off.

When you pay off the smallest debt, the payment from that debt plus any extra money you can come up with will go toward paying off the next one on your list—the second-smallest debt. Once you get your debt snowball rolling, you will begin to find money to throw toward your debt. Before you know it, the next one will be paid off.

When your first and second debts are both paid off, take the money you were using to pay toward those, plus any extra you can come up with, and begin throwing it at number three. After three is paid off, move on to four in the same way. Remember how we mentioned that good money management is 20 percent knowledge and 80 percent behavior? Starting with your smallest debts and working your way up without regard to the interest payments gives you quick wins that go a long way toward keeping you excited about modifying your behavior for good.

All the while, continue to make the minimum payment on all the debts except the smallest one you are currently working on. The genius in this is that every time you pay off a debt, the amount you pay on the next one increases. The money from old debts and any extra you can find by cutting your budget or selling things continues to go toward the next smallest debt until it is gone. The snowball gets bigger and bigger with every roll, knocking out the debt in its path.

A good, specific plan has a way of helping you line up your behavior with God's will for you. And it is definitely God's will for you to be out of debt. Now, the next step takes this even further.

Step 3: Decide to Do It in Half the Time

When you start your debt snowball, you can't know for sure how long it will take for you to pay everything off. But if you work through the math, you can get a pretty good idea. Think about money you can find in your budget to begin putting toward your debts. Combine that with what you're already paying. Factor in items you may be willing to sell and how far that money will go. Think through the snowball process, and estimate a date when you may finally be able to have your debt paid off. Depending on your situation, that target date may be two, five, or ten years from now. Once you have the date in mind, get alone with God, give it over to him, and pray:

God, I am committed to getting out of debt with this plan. I want to step away from constant financial pressure and walk in the freedom you have for me. I invite you and your power into this process. Help me to do it in half the time I think it will take.

You may remember my (Nelson's) personal story from the opening pages—you know, the one in which I realized my wife and I were in $22,000 of credit card debt in addition to outstanding educational debt. When we moved to New York to start a church, I couldn't shake the conviction that things needed to change. That period was truly the beginning of God working in my financial life in powerful ways.

I knew beyond a shadow of a doubt that God wanted me to get out of debt. At the same time, I was also convicted about my level of giving. I could feel God saying, "Nelson, you have got to get out of debt and honor me with what I've given you. I want to entrust you with the true riches of heaven. I want you to lead this new church and impact the city, but you have got to get your money under control." I could sense that God wouldn't be able to trust me with all he wanted to do in and through me if the financial area of my life remained so out of control.

So Kelley and I sat down, figured out exactly where we were financially, and set up a specific plan to get out of debt, which began with giving in order to break the bonds of consumerism in our lives. We entrusted that plan to God and then committed to doing it in half the time. I must confess that the idea of cutting the time in half wasn't mine. I'm not sure I'm bold enough to have thought of it. The concept came from a mentor friend of mine named Tom, who has helped thousands become debt-free. I distinctly remember hearing him challenge people like me to set up a plan and then, in bold faith, attempt to achieve the goal in half the time. His faith encouraged my faith—and exponentially sped up my debt-free journey. Thank you, Tom!

Over the next three years, Kelley and I worked our plan. We began living on less than we were making. We refused to add any new debt. We cut unnecessary expenses out of our monthly budget. We sold some things we didn't really need to free up cash, and we started packing all the extra money we could find into our debt snowball. God blessed our efforts tremendously. Several months ahead of the schedule we had sketched out, we were able to step out of debt once and for all. What a feeling! Then and there, we committed to living the rest of our lives debt-free.

Now Kelley and I have tremendous freedom to make decisions and take some risks that we wouldn't be able to make or take if we were still bound by debt. We continue to be excited tithers (as we have been since that initial decision to give first) and have the margin to invest in God's initiatives around the world in a way we never did when we were putting our money toward monthly debt payments and spinning our wheels to avoid sinking deeper into the hole. We have peace about money, the ability to save for the future, and the means to offer our son the gift of living in a family that's not dealing with constant financial stress. The benefits of being on this side of the debt equation are profound. If we can do it, you can too. Really.

Step 4: Do Your Part and Trust God to Do His Part

You can get out of debt by making the three decisions we covered in the last chapter—the three decisions Kelley and I made to begin our journey. *Decide to get out of debt. Live on less than you make. Add no new debt.* Once you've made those decisions, get started with the steps covered in this chapter. *Make a list of your liabilities and assets. Set up a repayment plan. Decide to do it in half the time.* The last step in this process is to do your part and trust God to do his.

In a letter Paul wrote to believers in the ancient Greek city of Ephesus, he closed with these words:

> Now all glory to God, who is able, through his mighty power at work within us, to accomplish infinitely more than we might ask or think. (Eph. 3:20)

When you put God first in any area of your life and trust him completely, he will bless that area. Things that may seem impossible to you are not impossible at all if they are infused with his power.

Being debt-free is a biblical mandate. Scripture clearly says that you should owe no person anything but your love (Rom. 13:8). Debt is not part of God's best plan for your life. He is more than willing to help you step out of crippling debt and into freedom as you commit your plan and your efforts to him.

Don't get discouraged! No matter how much debt you are in right now, you can do this. God is for you. Plan your work, and work your plan. And when the process gets tough, remember this promise:

> Let's not get tired of doing what is good. At just the right time we will reap a harvest of blessing if we don't give up. (Gal. 6:9)

CHAPTER 8

Capturing the Contentment Thief

How to Break Free from Materialism

GENEROSITY SECRET

Having more is not the answer.

For God is working in you, giving you the desire and the power to do what pleases him.

Philippians 2:13

M any years ago, there was a woman in Britain who loved collecting rare books. More than loved, actually—many would say she was obsessed with getting her hands on the oldest, rarest books she could find. She had an original copy of *The Great Gatsby*, several of Ernest Hemingway's earliest works, and even one of the first printings of *Pride and Prejudice*. During the day, she thought about how to get more books. At night, she dreamed about books. She scoured old, obscure bookstores and antique markets looking for her next treasure.

The woman had so many books that she had to clean out a room in her house to hold them. She even put a special padlock on the door so no one else could get in. Each time she got her hands on a new find, her process was the same. She'd drive home, tiptoe to the room holding her collection, unlock the padlock, rush in, close the door behind her, and carefully place the new book in its allocated spot.

Every time she did this, however, she was haunted by a strange presence. It was as if someone was whispering in her ear, "Margaret down the road has rarer books than you. Stephen has a bigger collection. If only you could get a few more gems, then you could be happy with your collection. You don't yet have enough." Occasionally, the whispering was even sinister. "Are you sure the padlock on your door is secure enough? What if Margaret tries to break in and steal one of your books?" Often when the whispering started, the woman thought she saw something, or someone, out of the corner of her eye. But when she turned to look, there was never anyone there.

One day, the woman stepped into her book room to deposit her latest acquisition and was pleased that she didn't sense the whispering. But she stopped in her tracks when she saw an impish little man standing by one of her stacks, holding a rare copy of *1984*, one she had never seen before. "Who are you?" she demanded. He replied that he was a thief. With that he placed the Orwell gently down on a stack and gave it a little dusting.

The man said, "Don't worry, this book isn't stolen. It's mine, and I'm giving it to you." As he spoke, the woman realized that his was the whispering voice she heard in her head each time she entered her book room.

"A thief!" she cried. "But if you are a thief, why did you bring a book to add to my collection rather than stealing from me? What kind of thief are you?"

"I don't want your books," the thief said. "You recognize my voice, don't you? I whisper to you about Margaret's collection and Stephen's collection. I cause you to worry about the safety of your collection. I persuade you that if you could just search out a few more rare finds, then you could be happy." The man continued, "I am here with you every time you set foot among your treasure, but I haven't come to steal your books, my lady. I have come to steal your contentment."[1]

The Contentment Thief

When you hear the word *materialism*, you probably associate it with someone other than yourself. You picture your brother-in-law who always has to have the latest gadgets or your friend from college who dresses in designer clothes you would never be able to buy. Materialism is one of those things that is easy to spot in others but hard to see in the mirror. In truth, we are all locked in a battle with materialism to some degree. It's almost impossible to avoid in our culture.

Materialism is simply an unhealthy desire to have more. It's not necessarily a money issue or a possessions issue; it's a heart issue. As we mentioned previously, it's a condition in which your heart is more preoccupied with material things than with spiritual things. Who among us hasn't been guilty of that? You won't be able to achieve long-term financial freedom until you get rid of any materialism that may have a grip on your heart. To help get there, let's bust three of the most common materialism myths.

Myth 1: Having more will make me happier.

The idea that more will bring happiness or contentment is an illusion. Just look around you. Some of the wealthiest people in the world are some of the most miserable. Money and possessions do not in themselves bring any lasting happiness.

Consider this: Psychological studies of lottery winners have shown the happiness that comes from winning the lottery lasts only about three months. After that, the new millionaires are no happier than they were before they won the lottery—and in many cases they are less happy. Why? Because we all get used to those material things that brought us pleasure so quickly. When we first get that raise, that new car, the new phone, or those boots we've been eyeing, it's exhilarating. But in no time at all, those things become our new normal and no longer bring the same level of happiness. Then the search for the next new thing begins all over again.

The truth is that having more money will just make you more of what you already are. Money is a magnifier. If you are discontent when you have a little bit of money, you will still be discontent when you have a lot of money. If you are unkind when you have a little bit of money, you will be tremendously unkind when you have a tremendous amount of money. That's why the truths and principles contained in these pages aren't simply about getting more money; they are about transforming your view of and relationship with money.

When you shift your financial paradigm and embrace the Generosity Secret, you begin to see money first and foremost as an opportunity for generosity. Then your money works to magnify that godly perspective. So if you use what money you have now generously, you will be even more generous when you have more money. If you happily support God's causes through his church with your current resources, you will be even more supportive when you have more to offer. Living from this place of generosity is what leads to true financial freedom and contentment.

Myth 2: Having more will make me more important.

One of the greatest fallacies we all grow up with is that we are what we own. Your value is not determined by your valuables. Until you drive this truth deeply into your heart, you will continue to buy things you don't need with money you don't have to impress people you may not even like. Having more does not make you more important. Most of the time it just puts you further in debt.

Myth 3: Having more will make me more secure.

Conventional wisdom says that having more money and more things provides security. That seems to make sense on the surface, doesn't it? When asked once, "How much money is enough money?" John D. Rockefeller is said to have replied, "Just a little bit more." We can all relate. But experience shows that the more money and possessions a person has, the more he or she becomes possessed by those possessions. There's constant worry about maintaining and protecting them. Oftentimes, having more makes people less secure, because the need to keep and grow what they have drives away any sense of security or contentment.

Having more will not make you happier. Having more will not make you more important. And having more will not make you more secure. Having more is not the path to financial freedom. If you think it is, then no matter how much you have, you will always feel like you need even more to be happy, even more to be important, and even more to be secure—and then more after that. You'll always be searching and striving. When materialism is at play, there is no finish line. There is no level that is finally enough. The only way to overcome the unending cycle of materialism is to learn to be content with what you currently have. Look at what Paul wrote on the subject:

> I have learned how to be content with whatever I have. I know how to live on almost nothing or with everything. I have learned the secret of living in every situation, whether it is with a full stomach or empty, with plenty or little. For I can do everything through Christ, who gives me strength. (Phil. 4:11–13)

Financial freedom will remain elusive until you decide to be content with your circumstances, no matter what they are. That doesn't mean you can't work hard and do better for yourself; you absolutely can. It means that your striving won't be in an effort to find happiness, worth, or security in your material possessions. Your happiness, worth, and security lie in something much better than wealth and possessions. They lie in God himself, through Jesus. When you know that truth and take it to heart, it doesn't matter how much you have or don't have. You will be able to be truly content in any and every circumstance.

The difficulty is that culture is constantly working against your contentment. The economy is powered by personal discontentment. By inundating you with images and reminders of things you don't have, it convinces you to be unhappy with what you do have. To be content with exactly what God has blessed you with is a countercultural way to live in a world that keeps pushing you toward more, better, newer. Just like the rare-book collector above, you have a thief whispering in your ear daily, "Just a little more. Just a little more and you'll be happy. You'll be important. You'll be secure. Just a little more."

The only way to shut the thief up is to learn how to make contentment an essential part of your makeup rather than just a nice idea. You have to fight for contentment every day and deposit your victories deep in your heart. Here are four strategies for making contentment tangible and learning to walk in its truth.

Four Strategic Keys to Contentment

1. Refuse to compare yourself with others.

Comparing yourself with others is always destructive. When you compare what you have—how much money you make, what kind of house you live in, where you go on vacation, what you drive, and what kind of clothes you wear—with that of the people around you, you are setting yourself up for inevitable disappointment and negativity. Even if you think you "win" in some of the categories or when measured against some people, you will "lose" in others and against others. And if comparison is your mindset, that loss will result in only resentment and envy. Have you ever found yourself thinking anything like the following thoughts?

- *Wow, look how big their house is. And their kitchen is brand-new. We need an upgrade.*
- *Her clothes are so much more stylish than mine. I have to go shopping and get some new things.*
- *When did he start driving that new model? Man, mine looks like a junker compared to that.*
- *They went to Disney World again and stayed on the property? We have to figure out how to get there soon or we'll be missing out.*

Comparison results in envy, and envy is spiritual and emotional poison. It can turn a person who is otherwise happy and content into someone who is miserable and discontent. Envy is also the catalyst for a lot of unwise financial decisions. It clouds judgment and causes you to spend money you shouldn't spend simply to keep up appearances for the people around you. This has been a problem since the beginning of time but has become turbo-charged in our social media culture. Psychology even has a term for it: *the social media comparison trap*. And that's exactly what it is—a trap.

To live a life of contentment, refuse to compare yourself to other people in any way. Comparison is natural, so this takes a lot of intentionality. But you can admire what others have without feeling the need to acquire the same thing or something better. After all, life is not a competition. When you feel envy rising up inside you over something someone else does or has, say to yourself, "I can admire without the need to acquire."

> "I can admire without the need to acquire."

As you make this your mantra, you will be able to compliment others on things they have that you don't, and really mean it. You will finally be able to celebrate other people's success, without the negative narrative of envy and need running in the background.

All you should be concerned with is learning to handle what God has given you in a way that pleases him. He has prepared your portion just for you. As you are trustworthy, he will trust you with more. Your wealth and your stuff are between you and God, just as Joe's down the street are between him and God. How silly to be comparing yourself to Joe. God is not doing the same things in and through Joe that he is doing in and through you. Joe's journey is his, and your journey is yours. You can't measure your success by a yardstick that belongs to someone else. In fact, Scripture tells you not to:

> Pay careful attention to your own work, for then you will get the satisfaction of a job well done, and you won't need to compare yourself to anyone else. For we are each responsible for our own conduct. (Gal. 6:4–5)

When God blesses other people, your immediate reaction should be "Yeah, God!" Then remind yourself of all the good things God is doing in your own life. Don't begrudge others what God has given them. Refuse to compare. Let go of envy. That's the first major key in being able to choose contentment.

2. Remember that life is not about stuff.

Materialism's greatest trick is causing you to start thinking that life is about things. Of course, you would never say that's what you believe. But your anxious thoughts, your constant striving, your tendency to compare . . . all of these are warning signs that you're buying into the lie.

While culture may scream otherwise, life is not about acquisition. Rather, it's about relationships—about learning to love God and love others. As long as you go through your days with an underlying sense that life is about stuff, you won't be able to focus on the love God is calling you to. Your priorities will be out of order and your perspective skewed. Your heart will follow your money, and your love for possessions will begin to outpace your love for God. The progression will be subtle, but slowly the things of God and his people will drop down your priority list. You'll find yourself spending more and more time thinking about your income, bills, toys, and trips than about God, your relationships with his people, and how you can engage with him in his work. Remember, money itself is not the root of all evil; the love of money is (1 Tim. 6:10).

The belief that life is about things also leads to the dangerous condition that God hates more than anything else— pride. When pride creeps into your heart, you begin to take credit for what God has done and blessed you with. You start seeing your possessions as a status symbol of how well you are doing. Pride says, "Look at me. Look at all I have. Look at what I earn. Look how good I am because I have more than you."

A prideful life is ultimately a miserable life. Your identity and your self-worth become wrapped up in your success, and sooner or later your success is going to fluctuate. Riches and possessions are fleeting. The winds will eventually shift despite your best efforts to keep them blowing your way. Who will you be then?

Proverbs 30:7–9 says this:

> O God, . . . give me neither poverty nor riches!
>   Give me just enough to satisfy my needs.
> For if I grow rich, I may deny you and say, "Who is
>   the LORD?"
>   And if I am too poor, I may steal and thus insult
>   God's holy name.

Financial freedom requires that you have the right relationship with your money and things, that you see them as the blessings from God that they are and as tools you can use for good. They are not the purpose of life. Material abundance will never be able to give you the meaning and significance that only God can give.

3. Start enjoying what you have.

Part of the fun of gift giving is watching the person you've given a gift to enjoy it. If you're a parent, you understand this truth. You love giving gifts to your kids. And it gets even better when you see them really enjoying something you've given them, right? So it is with God.

God blesses us with good things so that we can enjoy them. He doesn't want us to walk through life stressed about money and enduring our days. His plan for us is so much greater than that. He wants us to live life to the fullest. He wants us to rejoice in the people and things he has placed around us. As the author of Ecclesiastes wrote,

> And it is a good thing to receive wealth from God and the good health to enjoy it. To enjoy your work and accept your lot in life—this is indeed a gift from God. (5:19)

When your priorities are right and your heart is committed to his purposes, God has no problem with you enjoying the financial resources he has blessed you with. The problem comes when you can't enjoy what you have because you're too busy looking at what you want—what you think you need to finally make you happy.

Until you develop contentment, you'll be in danger of falling victim to what we like to call *when/then* thinking. *When/then* thinking sounds a little different for everyone, but the most common threads go something like this:

- *When we can move into a better neighborhood, then I'll be happy.*
- *When that promotion comes through, then I'll be happy.*
- *When we can put a pool in the backyard, then I'll be happy.*
- *When I don't have to drive this old car, then I'll be happy.*

- *When I can start earning more, then I'll be happy.*
- *When I get a bigger apartment, then I'll be happy.*
- *When I complete that home renovation, then I'll be happy.*
- *When I get my retirement funded, then I'll be happy.*
- *When I finally get to travel, then I'll be happy.*

The sad reality is that many people get to the end of their lives and realize they were never really happy because there was always another *when* that they had their eyes on. They were so busy thinking about what else they needed to be happy that they didn't enjoy the life God had given them. They wasted precious years—years that could have been spent enjoying the people and things around them—complaining about what they didn't have and always grasping for more.

One of the best ways to catch the contentment thief and send him packing is to learn to enjoy the life you've been given just as it is. Ask yourself, "What has God blessed me with that I'm not acting very thankful for?" Here are a few things you may be taking for granted:

- **Your current income**: Are you so worried about making more money that you aren't thankful for and enjoying what you have?

- **The home you live in**: Are you so dissatisfied with your current house or apartment that you take for granted all it offers you?

- **Your job**: Are you so focused on what you don't like about your job that you forget to be thankful you have a job in the first place?

- **The places you get to go with your family or friends**: Are you so distracted by the big trips you see others taking that you don't enjoy the adventures you do get to have with your loved ones?

Contentment is about being grateful for the place you're in and enjoying what you have, even if it doesn't feel like a lot. The truth is that God has already given you everything you need to enjoy your life. You can make the choice to be happy wherever you are, or you can choose to look at the things you don't have and walk around wishing your life away. But just as every parent knows, children who are grateful and engaged with what they have are much more likely to be blessed with even greater gifts than children who are constantly complaining and asking for more. Which child do you want to be?

4. Focus on what will last forever.

Whether it feels like it or not, your time on this earth is extremely short. All your working, striving, and accumulating is nothing but a small blip on the radar of eternity. It will be gone in the blink of an eye (Prov. 23:5). One of the best tools for learning to walk in daily contentment is to remind yourself to zoom out. Zoom out and look at your finances—actually, your entire life—from an eternal perspective. Will what you are working for and worrying about right now matter in fifty years, much less in eternity?

You may push back, arguing, "If I can build wealth now, I can set my family up to not have to struggle." Maybe. But will that money be more meaningful than the relationships you are sacrificing by working so many late nights? We're not saying you shouldn't work and work hard. You should. But where is your focus?

Is your focus on the money and the things that you think will bring security and contentment? As we have seen, wealth won't ultimately make you happy or give you security. Is your focus on making enough to get that boat or those season tickets or take that fourth European vacation? Again, there's nothing wrong with those things if they are not your priority. Is your focus on appearing successful in the eyes of the people around you? On proving how important you are? Remember, your worth comes from God and God alone, not from your money or your toys. Those things won't last.

There are only two things that will endure for eternity: your relationship with God and the relationships you create with other people. That's it. While money is a blessing and you are free to enjoy it, the most important decision you can make in your quest for contentment and financial freedom is to build your life on God rather than on the acquisition of stuff. You can lock the contentment thief up forever by deciding that loving God and loving people are more important than any financial level you may attain.

The thief may whisper, "More. More. You just need a little more." But God is whispering louder, "Trust me. I have given you all you have. Be trustworthy. Be content. Be generous with what I've given you, and I will bless you in ways you can't even imagine." Who will you choose to listen to?

Part 3

Living and Giving Differently

Hitting Your Stride

How to Walk in Step with God's Plan for Your Money

Tithing is key to your financial freedom.

Honor the LORD with your wealth
  and with the best part of everything you
    produce.
Then he will fill your barns with grain,
  and your vats will overflow with good wine.

Proverbs 3:9–10

Does the idea of the tithe make you uncomfortable? You aren't alone. The tithing issue is one of the most misunderstood and debated teachings in Christianity—but it's associated with truth that can't be ignored. Let's dig in and see what the Bible really has to say about the tithe and how it relates to your quest to get out of debt and walk in financial freedom.

In the last section, we discussed how the first step in getting out of debt is to give an initial gift to God. To put it another way, the first step in tapping into the Generosity Secret is to open your hand and give. As we mentioned, that's a good place to start but not a good place to stay. It is just the jumping-off point. Stalling after an initial stab at generosity would be like putting on your swimsuit, walking out to the pool, and spending all day with one toe in the water. You may have taken a step toward that crisp, fresh rush of immersion, but you stopped short of the reward. Once you have given your initial gift, it's time to go deeper. The next step is to begin regularly giving a percentage of your income in a way that honors God—or to begin tithing. This is the point at which you start being fully obedient to God with your finances.

The number of self-professing followers of Jesus who have never studied the concept of the tithe continually amazes us. They may have listened to what other people—including financially stressed relatives, coworkers, and friends—have said about the tithe but have never taken the time to dig into Scripture and see for themselves what it is all about.

Even in the midst of rampant ignorance, if you want to start an argument in Christian circles, bring up tithing. Few topics ignite the same kind of heated discussion. Why? Well, first of all, there's that inseparable link between a person's money and his heart (Matt. 6:21), so any dialogue dealing with the handling of personal finances strikes at the core of our being. As such, the differing viewpoints on giving are all charged by passion. Everyone's opinion is attached to their checkbook, so their hearts are engaged. Let's see if we can find some clarity.

Engaging with the Generosity Secret

Take a look at one of the most famous giving passages ever written. Addressing the people of Israel, God says,

> "Will a mere mortal rob God? Yet you rob me.
> "But you ask, 'How are we robbing you?'
> "In tithes and offerings. You are under a curse—your whole nation—because you are robbing me. Bring the whole tithe into the storehouse, that there may be food in my house. Test me in this," says the LORD Almighty, "and see if I will not throw open the floodgates of heaven and pour out so much blessing that there will not be room enough to store it." (Mal. 3:8–10 NIV)

In this passage, God clues us all in to three important truths about the tithe. First of all, if we are not tithing, we are robbing him. Partial obedience is complete disobedience. That's why you can't give an initial gift and then think you're good to go. While it's a necessary first step, it's not yet in the realm of obedience.

Can you imagine if a husband approached his wife and asked, "Honey, have you been faithful to me?" and she replied, "Well, partially. I've only cheated on you twelve out of the last fifty-two weeks." That wouldn't work, would it? Partial obedience is complete disobedience.

Before we go any further, let's define the tithe, just to ensure clarity. A tithe literally means the first tenth. You are commanded to return one tenth of your income back to God—but not just any tenth. You are to give back the first tenth of all God blesses you with each time you are paid.

> Honor the LORD with your possessions,
> And *with the firstfruits of all your increase*;
> So your barns will be filled with plenty,
> And your vats will overflow with new wine.
> (Prov. 3:9–10 NKJV, emphasis added)

Giving leftovers won't do. God wants the best of what you— and we—have to offer.

Early in the pages of Scripture, there's an interesting story about two brothers named Cain and Abel. God comes to the two brothers and asks them to bring him an offering. Abel, who is a shepherd, immediately brings the best of the firstborn lambs from his flock and sacrifices it before God. But Cain, a farmer by trade, approaches God's request with quite a different attitude.

> When it was time for the harvest, Cain presented some of his crops as a gift to the LORD. (Gen. 4:3)

While the Lord is pleased with Abel's gift, Cain's gift is not acceptable. In fact, God says to him,

> You will be accepted if you do what is right. But if you refuse to do what is right, then *watch out*! (Gen. 4:7, emphasis added)

What was the difference? Abel immediately brought God the first of his increase. Cain, when he was ready, brought

God *some* of his increase. What you give God and when you give it is a testament to the ordering of your heart's priorities. You definitely don't want to be on the receiving side of God's *watch out*!

The story of these two brothers also illustrates that those who are not tithing are not living with God's full blessing. The Scriptures are clear that those who aren't honoring God financially are actually under a curse. In other words, failing to tithe blocks God's ability to bless us to the extent he would like to. That's a tough pill to swallow, isn't it?

What does this curse look like in today's culture? Here are a few of the trademark symptoms:

- Going to bed every night worried about money.
- Arguing with your spouse over money.
- Being unable to save or enjoy money the way God intended.
- Feeling guilty that you aren't making a difference for others with your money.
- Being unable to support God's mission in your church and the world as you would like to.
- Spending too much time thinking about money.
- Living in fear of losing your money or things.

No one can mock God. You can't expect to ignore and dispute his plan for your livelihood and yet continue to walk with his blessing on your life. But when you are obedient to the call to tithe, he will bless you in unimaginable ways—both financially and otherwise. We have learned firsthand that we would rather tithe 10 percent and live with God's supernatural blessing on the other 90 percent than to have the full 100 percent in our pocket but operate without God's blessing. The fear of living without God's hand in your finances should be greater than the fear of giving a portion back to him and his work.

On a side note, one of the questions we most frequently hear about tithing is, "Should I tithe off of my gross income or my net income?" Our answer is always the same: "Which amount do you want God to bless?" When you make a decision to tithe off of your net income, you are essentially putting the government in a position of priority over God. You are giving to him off of what's left after Uncle Sam steps in and takes his due. Giving based on what the government leaves behind is not a tithe.

This Is a Test

Take another look at the passage in which God is teaching the Israelites about giving:

> "Will a mere mortal rob God? Yet you rob me.
>
> "But you ask, 'How are we robbing you?'
>
> "In tithes and offerings. You are under a curse—your whole nation—because you are robbing me. Bring the whole tithe into the storehouse, that there may be food in my house. *Test me in this*," says the LORD Almighty, "and see if I will not throw open the floodgates of heaven and pour out so much blessing that there will not be room enough to store it." (Mal. 3:8–10 NIV, emphasis added)

This is the only place in all of Scripture where God says "test me" in a positive way. He is essentially saying, "Bring me

134

the tithe and see if I don't bless you. Go ahead. Try it." His challenge here is to Christians and non-Christians alike.

At the church I (Nelson) pastor, The Journey Church, we sometimes put out a tithe challenge for our people, and we direct it at both believers and nonbelievers. Here's how it works: I teach our people what God says about the tithe, as we've been discussing here, and then ask them to test God in his promise by committing to tithe for a short period of time, usually four months.

In issuing the challenge, I will go so far as to say, "Hey, if you don't believe in God, isn't it worth a little bit of your income over the next few months to prove once and for all he doesn't exist? You are staking your eternity on this, so why not? Why don't you tithe for four months and if you still think God doesn't exist, you can live the rest of your life without having to worry about it."

God said to test him.

One time, there was a gentleman at The Journey who was a self-professed agnostic. Let's call him Ben. Ben happened to be visiting with a friend one fall Sunday when I laid out this tithe challenge. Now, Ben was a little older than our average attenders, and he was in the midst of a successful career as an air traffic controller.

> "I never would have been able to tithe the first million dollars I ever made if I had not tithed my first salary, which was $1.50 per week."
> —John D. Rockefeller

After the service, Ben came over to me and said, "Okay. I'm going to test God. I want to take this 'tithe challenge' and dispel all of this foolishness. I'm going to prove to you that God doesn't exist." So he and I sat down and figured out what 10 percent of his gross income would be and divided that out over the next four months. He came to church a couple of times during the course of the challenge, but not regularly. His tithing, however, was like clockwork. Can you guess what happened?

Ben began being blessed both tangibly and intangibly. God worked in his life in amazing ways. To make a long story short, Ben came back to me after those four months fully convinced of God's existence. Of course, as usually happens when someone takes the tithe challenge, he has continued to tithe.

Ben is not an exception to the rule. I have seen this scenario play out time and time again. God shows up in people's lives when they honor him. He has obligated himself to. God's promise about tithing is an *if/then* promise: *If you will honor me with your first of your increase, then I will pour out my blessing in your life. Test me.*

Remember the similar challenge Paul gave to the Corinthian church—the challenge we are working toward: "Since you excel in so many ways—in your faith, your gifted speakers, your knowledge, your enthusiasm, and your love from us—I want you to excel also in this gracious act of giving" (2 Cor. 8:7). Ten percent is just the threshold. As we excel in grace, we should excel in giving.

One of the rebuttals we often hear is not on the amount of a God-honoring gift but on where it should be given. Some people believe they should be able to distribute their tithe as they see fit. If they aren't happy with the way their local church handles its finances, they think they should have the freedom to give their tithe to an outside organization. But Scripture teaches us that the tithe is to go to the local church—the one and only organization that is eternal. Offerings, any giving over and above the tithe, can be given outside the church, but the tithe can't.

In Malachi 3, God says to bring the whole tithe into the storehouse. Why? So that *"there may be food in my house."* In biblical times, the storehouse referred to the temple. Today, it is the modern church. The food that God refers to is the ministry of the temple or, as we understand it, the ongoing work of God through his church on this earth.

The tithe is specifically intended to infuse the local church so that God's kingdom can continue to expand at the best possible rate. It is not up to us as givers to judge where we'd like to give our tithe. We are simply told to make it the firstfruits, make it proportional, and bring it to the storehouse.

When you begin to be obedient by bringing the full tithe back to God, you move from being under the curse into the blessing zone. You put yourself in a position for God to be able to pour his blessing into your life . . . for him to begin replacing your financial stress with financial peace as you open your hand to him.

Tithing is about priority. When you bring the tithe back to God—which, by the way, is exactly what you are doing; it is his to begin with—you are saying, "God, you are more important than money. You are bigger than money. You have first place in my life." Putting God first in your finances throws open the door to a life of blessing.

Once you experience how this level of generosity changes your life, you'll never want to go back to closefisted living. If you wear eyeglasses or contacts, this may be a little like the first time you put on a pair of glasses or put in a pair of contacts that were the right prescription for you. Weren't

Tithing Worksheet

Ten percent sounds like an easy number to come up with, but many people never actually think through what their full tithe should be. Take a minute to complete this worksheet so you will know how to begin honoring God by returning the first 10 percent of your income to him.

How much do I make in a year (before taxes)? $_____
My yearly tithe should be (10 percent): $_____
How much do I make in a month (before taxes)? $_____
My monthly tithe should be (10 percent): $_____

you shocked by how clear and beautiful the world around you suddenly looked? Before, you probably didn't even realize you couldn't see clearly. But once you experienced the world through the proper lens, you knew you could never go back to the blur.

In all our years of helping people embrace the Generosity Secret, we have never, ever had anyone say to us, "You know, tithing was a bad decision. I wish I'd never taken that step." Time and time again, we hear stories about how people are living more blessed lives on 90 percent of their income than they ever could have dreamed of living on 100 percent. If you want to know that God exists, start tithing. If you want God's blessing on your finances, start tithing.

GENEROSITY SECRET

Stop debating the tithe and just test it.
You'll know in a few months if it's worth it.

The Tithing Debate

Some of you may be interested in diving a little deeper into the debate that tithing opponents like to engage in. In broad terms, the divide over tithing comes down to an examination of legalism versus grace.

Opponents say that tithing, which has been in existence since the beginning of humankind (Gen. 14:20; Lev. 27:30–33) and was a command of the Jewish law (Num. 18:28–29; Deut. 12:11), was abolished when Jesus stepped on the scene. But Scripture confirms that Jesus came to earth to fulfill the law—not to dismiss it. Jesus himself minces no words when he says this:

> Don't misunderstand why I have come. I did not come to abolish the law of Moses or the writings of the prophets. No, I came to accomplish their purpose. I tell you the truth, until heaven and earth disappear, not even the smallest detail of God's law will disappear until its purpose is achieved. So if you ignore the least commandment and teach others to do the same, you will be called the least in the Kingdom of Heaven. But anyone who obeys God's laws and teaches them will be called great in the Kingdom of Heaven. (Matt. 5:17–19)

Jesus shifted the heart of humanity from legalism to grace, but in doing so, he in no way rendered the law obsolete.

You are probably familiar with Jesus's most famous teaching, the Sermon on the Mount (Matt. 5–7). Even if you've never read the account for yourself, you likely know a lot about what he says in it. The words have integrated themselves into the foundation of our Western civilization. In this teaching,

Jesus magnifies rather than minimizes the expectations that had previously been associated with the law of Moses.

He says, and we paraphrase, "You've heard that you shouldn't murder. Well, I say don't even be angry with anyone. You know that you shouldn't commit adultery, but guess what? Under grace, you have already done so if you even look at a woman lustfully" (Matt. 5:21–22, 27–28). The expectations that Jesus places on his followers, thanks to the introduction of grace, go above and beyond the expectations of the law that preceded him.

If anger is now on the level with murder and lust on the level with adultery, doesn't it stand to reason that the tithe would now be considered a base-level command—a minimum expectation now maximized through grace, like the other components of the law? Much to the contrary of being obsolete, giving under grace implies that we should all be giving even more sacrificially than those who gave under the law; we should be operating at a higher level than the threshold that was previously mandated.

Even under the bondage of the law, devout Jews often took it upon themselves to give God more than the first 10 percent of their increase. They certainly weren't begrudging. They recognized the truth of the Generosity Secret's foundational paradigm shift—that all they had came from God. And they understood the command to return their first and best to him.

Logic then suggests that all of us who have been given so much would also recognize the source of our blessings and feel even more inclined to return the tithe as an act of worship. After all, that's what tithing truly is; it's an act of worship. We should easily recognize 10 percent as simple obedience—like we recognize not murdering and not committing adultery as simple obedience—and be filled with the desire to give at least that much. Unfortunately, this is not always the case.

Under grace, the average modern-day Christian gives only 2.5 percent of his or her income, which, obviously, is nowhere close to a tithe. As one author notes,

> When we as New Testament believers, living in a far more affluent society than ancient Israel, give only a fraction of that given by the poorest Old Testament believers, we surely must reevaluate our concept of "grace giving." And when you consider that we have the indwelling of the Spirit of God and they didn't, the contrast becomes even more glaring.[1]

We seem to have a heart problem. Could the problem be that, deep down, many of those who oppose the tithe do so not out of biblical scouring, prayer, and deduction but out of misinformation or their own sinful (perhaps even subconscious) desire to be the master of their own money? To hold it and do with it as they wish?

Their hearts are tied to their wallets, as are all of ours. When the contents of those wallets aren't being poured into God's work, it makes sense that their hearts—far from understanding the supernatural blessings associated with the practical funding of God's kingdom—are waging a war for financial control.

As a result, they fight against the tithe. They call tithing outdated and legalistic. Even if only subconsciously, they feel that if they can discount the biblical mandate for twenty-first-century Jesus followers to tithe, then they can continue to handle their money as they please. The majority of these people do not intentionally choose to be selfish. They are just caught up in a problem of the heart—one that is often caused more by lack of knowledge about the tithe than by willful disobedience. Think of your fifty-dollar bill with the heart pinned on top. The heart is pinned on top of the bill, not the other way around. Those who oppose the tithe are in essence taking the bill and placing it on top of the heart, making money the victor over a heart dedicated to God's purposes. The above observation continues:

> The Israelites' tithes [often] amounted to 23% of their income—in contrast to the average 2.5% giving of American Christians. This statistic suggests that the law was about ten times more effective than grace! Even using 10% as a measure, the Israelites were four times more responsive to the Law of Moses than the average American Christian is to the grace of Christ.[2]

Let that sink in. Do you think that's what Jesus intended when he said that he didn't come to abolish the law but to accomplish it? He calls us to go deeper and higher in our pursuit of God's desires—not to use his presence as an excuse to fall beneath the bar set by the law.

Tithing opponents rely most heavily on the argument that we are all free from the law, that we have the liberty of giving to the God of our salvation through grace, and that is a true argument. One hundred percent undeniable. But a piece of the puzzle they are trying to put together is missing. While they purport tithing as legalism, modern Christians are, by and large, living lives of stress and struggle. Our finances are out of control. We never seem to have enough, so we eagerly buy into their claim that we don't have to tithe. That means more for us, right? Wrong. The missing puzzle piece begins to take shape with Jesus's words:

> You should tithe, yes, but do not neglect the more important things. (Matt. 23:23)

Jesus addresses tithing as something so understood that it's almost unworthy of a mention. You are free from the law, yes. But you have been called to live by the higher standard of grace.

Sometimes we all just need to take a step back and examine why we believe the way we do. What substantiates our positions? How do they measure up with God's reality?

The Blessing Zone

When you begin tithing, God's spiritual laws kick into high gear. Since you are honoring him, he honors you. His blessings may not always be tangible. This isn't a give-to-get-financial-blessing scenario. But they will be there, tangible and intangible.

People who tithe have more money left at the end of the month than people who don't. People who tithe are able to pay off credit card debt and student loans faster. They have peace and security when difficult financial times hit. They are able to save for the future and for their children's education. God's Word is true. *Test me in this.*

People often say to us, "I'm praying about whether or not I should tithe." Well, we don't want to discourage anyone from praying, so go ahead and pray. But, like on so many other issues, Jesus has already given the answer. *Of course you should tithe* (Matt. 23:23). If only all prayers were so easily answered!

In my (Nelson's) office, I have a file cabinet full of testimonies from people who have taken the tithe challenge and have seen God's promise of blessing become a reality. Here are just a few of those:

I had been distant from my parents and knew I needed to go home to visit. I make pretty good money, but because of my debt there was no way I could manage the trip. Although travel at my level of the company I work for never happens, my company sent me on a trip soon after I took the tithing challenge. Where did they send me? To the town where my parents live!—AR

When you asked us to take the tithing challenge, my first thought was, "Yeah, right!" I work at a restaurant and just barely make ends meet. I knew it was the right thing to do, though, so I took the challenge. Soon after, I got the job that I had been pursuing for over six months.—AH

I don't have any stories about how money for something I really needed suddenly appeared. I think the best thing that has come out of this is that God has given me the strength to really see that I already have so much and should take the time to appreciate what I do have.—CC

Since I took the tithing challenge, I have really stuck with it and God truly has blessed me! Before, when I would tithe (or try to), I would always skimp short because I was afraid of not having money to make ends meet if I gave up that money. Since I have been tithing, I have really just put my faith in God and he has completely come through, and then some! I definitely plan to complete the challenge and to continue tithing even when it's over. This has really opened my eyes to just have faith in God to take care of things that I can't control. I'm trying to do the same thing in other areas of my life too.—SN

God has been really testing my faith in ways that I never would have thought since committing to tithing. I have actually had trial after trial, from finances to my job to my personal life. But God has grown my faith a great deal. And although it has hurt more than a little, my faith has grown more than I would have imagined.—LC

Within one week of making the commitment to honor God with my finances, I was given an amazing career advancement opportunity with an annual raise of about 25 percent.—CJ

These people embraced the Generosity Secret, took the tithe challenge, and opened themselves up to a life of blessing. Are you ready to do the same? If you are, it's as easy as simply getting started. You may want to tell your pastor what you are doing, but you don't have to. Just begin tithing and then continue as you began. The four-month tithe challenge is just the right amount of time for you to begin seeing God's hand at work all around you. When you do, you'll never want to go back to your old way of giving.

CHAPTER 10

The 70 Percent Principle of Lasting Wealth

How to Set Goals for Giving, Saving, and Investing

GENEROSITY SECRET

Tell your money where to go, and you'll never have to wonder where it went.

Seek the Kingdom of God above all else, and live righteously, and he will give you everything you need.

Matthew 6:33

The late, great Christian entrepreneur Jim Rohn tells the story of an early encounter with his mentor in life, a gentleman named Earl Shoaff. According to Mr. Rohn, he sat down to breakfast early one morning with Mr. Shoaff to talk about where Mr. Rohn was in life and what he wanted for his future. The conversation went something like this:

> Mr. Shoaff: *Jim, let me see your list of goals. Let's go over them and talk about them. Maybe that's the best way I can help you right now.*
>
> Mr. Rohn: *I don't have a list.*
>
> Mr. Shoaff: *Well, is it out in the car or at home somewhere?*
>
> Mr. Rohn: *No, sir, I don't have a list anywhere.*
>
> Mr. Shoaff: *Well, young man, that's where we better start. If you don't have a list of your goals, I can guess your bank account within a few hundred dollars.* (And then he did, which got Mr. Rohn's attention.)
>
> Mr. Rohn: *You mean, if I had a list of goals, that would change my bank balance?*
>
> Mr. Shoaff: *Drastically.*[1]

Goal setting is powerful. In fact, it's essential to living life with intentional direction rather than being carried along by the current of your weeks, months, and years. Without goals, we all drift. We become concerned with whatever is in front of us that seems urgent at the moment, to the exclusion of the things that may ultimately be the most important. This applies to your money as much as it does to anything else.

When you think about your financial future, you probably experience one of two emotions: fear or excitement. Some level of fear grips most people. Does it have its claws in you? A lack of planning is the main thing that fuels the fear. When you don't have a plan in place for your future, you end up afraid of what the future might hold, whether you will have enough, whether you are able to be and do the things you want to be and do. A clear plan is the best antidote to your fear.

> A clear plan is the best antidote to your fear.

In your quest to get out of debt and take hold of the Generosity Secret by becoming an obedient giver, you'll need to set up a specific plan for telling your money where to go. As the old adage says, if you don't tell your money where to go, you'll wind up wondering where it went. To help, we have developed a principle that has a plan for your finances built right into it.

The principle we are about to present summarizes much of what the Bible teaches about financial freedom. If you follow the plan inherent in this principle, it will set you up not only for immediate financial health but also for lasting wealth. It pushes you to get your priorities right and allocate your money in a wise, God-honoring way. This principle alone, if taken seriously, will revolutionize your financial world. Are you ready?

The 70 Percent Principle of Lasting Wealth— A God-Honoring Plan for Financial Freedom

- The **first** 10 percent of your income goes back to God as a **tithe.**
- The **second** 10 percent of your income goes to **debt or savings.**
- The **third** 10 percent of your income goes to **savings or investments.**

Let's break it down:

The first 10 percent goes back to God as a tithe. Opening your hand from around your finances and being quick to offer back to God the first 10 percent of any income you receive is the foundation of lasting wealth. God wants you to build on this truth, as we explored in the last chapter. When you consider how few people in America tithe their income, it's no surprise that so many people are in extreme debt or that bankruptcy is at an all-time high. Those things are natural results of violating this very first component of the 70 Percent Principle of Lasting Wealth.

The second 10 percent goes to debt or savings. If you are in debt, the second 10 percent of your income goes toward paying off your debt. This is what you can throw toward your debt snowball. If you need a refresher on how the debt snowball works, turn back to chapter 7. If you are already out of debt, congratulations! You now get to take a major step toward securing your financial freedom. As soon as your paycheck comes in, put the second 10 percent of your income into savings.

Modern Americans are terrible at saving money. According to one source, in the event of a job loss or major unexpected expense, the average family is three-to-six weeks away from bankruptcy.[2] That's a frightening statistic. How does it line up with your reality? If your income stopped, how long would you be able to live on your savings? Financial advisors recommend having at least six months of living expenses saved. Yet most people don't have anywhere close to that amount of

money saved—which means that unexpected circumstances can create major catastrophes. Saving money
requires the discipline to say no to our financial whims,
choosing instead to look toward what we will need or
enjoy more in the future.

Keep in mind, there's a major difference between saving for future needs, dreams, and goals and hoarding,
or saving out of greed. When you save in the systematic
way that the 70 Percent Principle recommends, you are
first buffering yourself against unexpected events or
emergencies. You are giving yourself wise margin in
your finances. Once you have about six months of living
expenses saved, then you can start tagging your savings
in other ways. Maybe you want to save for a family vacation you've always dreamed of, a remodeling project,
or your kids' college educations. The point is that you
live with an eye toward future expenses and continually put money aside to prepare for those expenses in
the present rather than allowing them to put you in a
financial bind in the future.

The third 10 percent goes to savings or investments. If you
are in debt, the second 10 percent of your income goes
toward your debt, and the third 10 percent goes toward
saving in the way we just discussed. But if you are out
of debt and the second 10 percent is going toward your
savings, things begin to get exciting. Now you can take
that third 10 percent off the top of your income and
begin investing wisely.

Investing for your future—not to mention investing
to expand your ability to give to God's kingdom—is
part of being a wise financial steward. But as with

everything else money related, the condition of your heart is key here. There are good reasons to invest and not-so-good reasons to invest. When you invest sensibly and with the right heart, investing is a crucial part of your overall plan for financial freedom. Here are a few good reasons to grow your money through smart investments:

- To be able to provide for yourself during your later years
- To pay for your children's educations
- To leave an inheritance for your family
- To take the Generosity Secret up another level by giving even more to God
- To have financial freedom that allows more of your time and money to be used to accomplish God's purposes in your own circle of influence and around the world

On the other side of the coin, again, you should never invest out of greed or pride. Your motivation should not be to get more and more in an attempt to impress others or find some elusive level of happiness. As Paul wrote,

> People who long to be rich fall into temptation and are trapped by many foolish and harmful desires that plunge them into ruin and destruction. (1 Tim. 6:9)

Make wise investments from a heart bent on creating a strong foundation for the future, on being able to take care of yourself and loved ones during later years of life, and on having money available to give and serve more. Then you will be investing that third 10 percent in a way that God is happy to honor and that brings a great return.

In chapter 6, we talked about deciding to live on less money than you make. The 70 Percent Principle of Lasting Wealth gives that decision some handles you can hold on to. It's no longer a vague notion of learning to leave margin in your finances but a specific goal of living on 70 percent of what you make.

You may be thinking, *If I earned more money, I could do that*. But this principle is not contingent on making more money. Rather, it hinges on getting your priorities in line and discovering the peace that comes from being content with what you have and where you are right this minute. Until you learn to live on 70 percent of what you are making right now, you will not be putting yourself in a position where God can bless you well with more.

If you think living on 70 percent sounds difficult, you may need to begin disciplining yourself in small ways. Set some goals for your spending as well. Again, budgeting is an important part of your financial freedom, as we've discussed, but this moves beyond budgeting and strikes at the heart of self-control. As Paul wrote to early believers,

Teach the [others] to be temperate, worthy of respect, self-controlled, and sound in faith, in love and in endurance. (Titus 2:2 NIV)

Having self-control in the area of spending, especially, is paramount to your ability to live on 70 percent of your income and create a generous life.

Over time, small, everyday decisions can have a major impact on your financial life. By taking the initiative to examine your spending habits and figure out where your money is going, you can identify the areas that would most benefit from daily discipline. For example, not long ago, I (Nelson) started paying closer attention to my lunch habits. I was surprised by what I found. I had been stepping out of the office for a sandwich or salad for lunch almost every day. Given my location, a typical lunch cost me anywhere from $11 to $15. When I started adding up the cost, I realized I was spending about $200 per month on lunch. That's more than $2,600 every year, $8000 over three years.

Seeing the actual price tag for my lunches made me realize I was throwing money away. Instead of continuing to go with the flow and watch my income disappear, I decided to start bringing my lunch to work. After all, I could make a sandwich at home for about a dollar. Once I understood what kind of money I could save by brown bagging, my homemade sandwiches started tasting more delicious than anything I could buy in a restaurant. This simple discipline helped with my budget and freed up money in my account that needed to be used for more important things.

What habits do you have that are slowly depleting your bank account? Do you spend $4 on a cup of coffee every day? That adds up to $124 every month, $1,460 per year. What could you do with that extra $1,460 if you started brewing your coffee at home? If you are in debt, you could start paying off what you owe. If you are ready to invest for the future, there's almost $1,500 you didn't have last year; you could add it to an existing money market account and start earning higher dividends. Or you could keep sweetening it with cream and sugar and drinking it down. Your small financial decisions—whether wise or otherwise—will slowly shape your financial future.

If you were to interview the wealthiest people in America, you may be surprised to find that many of them are the kind of people who eat humble lunches. They drink their own coffee. They drive slightly older cars. Studies show that the vast majority of wealthy people are not extravagant. Rather, they make small exchanges every day to ensure they stay on the path to wealth.

Your initial reaction may be to think of this kind of spending discipline as painful. In reality, it brings freedom—freedom from the stress of debt, the fear of not having enough, and the weight of poor financial management. As you take steps toward discipline, keep in mind the purpose behind what you are doing, and the perceived pain will shift accordingly. Maybe you've already experienced a financial crisis as the result of not living a disciplined life in the past. Don't let yourself forget that. Let that pain become your purpose for choosing discipline from here on out.

> So let's not get tired of doing what is good. At just the right time we will reap a harvest of blessing if we don't give up. (Gal. 6:9)

Automate Everything

Now that you have some clearly defined goals for giving, saving, and investing your income, we want to give you a tip that can help you stay on track even when you don't feel like it or don't think you can: *automate everything!* Automate all the financial outflow you can automate, beginning with your giving.

Once you understand the power of the Generosity Secret—that generous giving leads to financial freedom—there's no reason *not* to automate your giving. After all, you know you want to give to God's work regularly and off the top of your income, so why not set up a system for making sure you don't forget or fall behind? Given the fact that you can't give without receiving God's blessing in return, doesn't it make sense to protect yourself from missing out on that blessing?

Years ago, I (Nelson) read a book about financial management that strongly suggested automating the key financial areas of my life. The argument the author made was hard to ignore. At the time, I was renting an apartment, so I automated my rent. Now I have a small mortgage, so I automate that. I have most of my bills set up to pay automatically. But most importantly, I automate the top 30 percent of my income. When I have money come in, my giving, saving, and investing all come out automatically. What I'm left with is the 70 percent I want to use to live on.

Of all the things I automate, though, my giving is by far the most important—and it is the most important thing you can automate as well. When something matters to you, you prioritize it. You make sure it doesn't fall through the cracks. If you are in a relationship with God, and he has shown you the value of honoring him with your money, then you will find great freedom and joy in ensuring you are being obedient to the type of giving he has called you to.

If you are on a regular salary, it's simple to automate your giving. Set it up so that your tithe comes out as soon as you get paid. If you work on commission or have an irregular salary, you can still do the same. You may just need to auto-mate a small amount to give every week that adds up to the percentage you've committed to God. Or you may want to set a reminder on your phone to give as soon as your check comes in.

Today, most churches make giving regular, automated gifts very simple. Check with your local church to see if there's an app you can give through or a way to set up automatic giving online. Automating your giving is all about committing to consistency, and the true blessing of giving comes through such consistency.

Small-Step Alternative

If living on 70 percent of your income is simply too big of a leap for you right now, there is a way to take a smaller step toward this principle. We don't teach it often because we don't want anyone to get stuck in this place. Still, we would rather you adopt the habit that is foundational to the prin-ciple and build on it than throw your hands up in frustration over the percentage. So here is a small-step alternative to the 70 Percent Principle of Lasting Wealth. If you feel like this option would allow you to start getting your finances in order quickly and in a more sustainable way, begin here. Then work your way up as quickly as possible.

The small-step alternative is called the 88 Percent Principle of Lasting Wealth. With this plan, you commit to living on 88 percent of your income, tithing 10 percent, saving 1 per-cent, and investing 1 percent. Notice the tithe doesn't change. That percentage is key to your financial freedom. But the percentage you save and invest increases more slowly. Again, we recommend taking the leap to the 70 Percent Principle of Lasting Wealth right away, but if that principle is going to scare you into inaction, then take this small step first. When you have lived with the 88 Percent Principle of Lasting Wealth for a little while and feel more secure in your financial standing, adjust those percentages to reflect the true principle.

To step into the financial future you want, you have to have well-defined goals—goals for giving, saving, and investing in a wise, God-honoring way. The 70 Percent Principle of Lasting Wealth is your ongoing framework for those goals. Put it into practice, and it will pull you forward into a future you can continually view with excitement rather than fear.

The 70 Percent Principle of Lasting Wealth

Imagine that a sum of money (like your paycheck!) comes into your life. What do you do? First of all, you don't close your fist around it; you keep your hand open and thank God for it. Then you tell it where to go:

If you are not in debt . . .

- The first 10 percent goes to your **tithe.**
- The second 10 percent goes into **savings.**
- The third 10 percent goes toward **investments**.

If you are in debt . . .

- The first 10 percent goes to your **tithe.**
- The second 10 percent goes to pay off **debt**.
- The third 10 percent goes into **savings**.

One of the major keys to reaching financial freedom is this: **Learn to live on 70 percent of your income.**

CHAPTER 11

Living beyond the 70 Percent

How to Embrace the Full Power of the Generosity Secret

GENEROSITY SECRET

You were born to live a generous life.

And I am praying that you will put into action the generosity that comes from your faith as you understand and experience all the good things we have in Christ.

Philemon 1:6

Do you know your purpose? Do you know why you are here? Is it to build a career? A family? What wakes you up each morning and inspires you to face the day with expectation? For too many, the answer is simply *nothing*. Or *obligation*. Or *the need to put food on the table*. But that's not how God intended for you to live.

Have you ever read about, or seen firsthand, how a swallow teaches her young to fly? First, she gathers all of her chicks into a line and then begins pushing them toward the end of a high tree branch. Eventually the one at the front of the line falls off. Even though that little chick is surely surprised and scared at first, it instinctively pumps its little wings and begins to fly. This scenario repeats itself over and over until all the chicks are off the branch and flying on their own.

Sometimes, however, there's a stubborn chick that won't let go of the branch. When this happens, the mother swallow pecks at the little chick's talons with her beak until the chick's pain outweighs its fear of flying. In that moment, the willful little chick finally lets go, pumps its wings, and soars—just as birds are designed to do.

In a similar way, fear of the unknown and fear of not having enough has the potential to keep you from taking the leap into the life you were created to live. You were born with an innate spirit of ever-increasing generosity, as much as those baby birds were born with an innate sense of flight. You were born to live a generous life. This may be a new realization for you. Or maybe you've felt that truth pecking at your heart for years, but you have also felt a very real sense of accompanying fear. So you've held on to your branch for dear life. Hopefully now you're beginning to realize that the pain of financial stress caused by closefisted living is worse than taking the leap into a new, better way of doing things.

When you discover how to live generously, you are free to soar into the life of blessing that God wants you to have. But how do you let go of the safety of the branch? How do you truly flex your wings and fly? By discovering the exhilaration and freedom found in living beyond the 70 percent. In other words, by stepping into your identity as a generous giver.

Upping the Generous of the Generosity Secret

You reach the top level of the inherent power of the Generosity Secret by becoming a generous giver. This means acknowledging the pull toward openhandedness within you and leaping into a generous life—not a life of disobedience and not a life of minimum requirements but a life running over with the spirit of generosity. A generous life is characterized by three main things:

1. **A willingness to stretch yourself:** Instead of giving the minimum tithe, you stretch yourself to take even larger steps of faith. You ask yourself, *What kind of giver does God want me to be? Is he stretching you to give 11 or 12 percent? Or maybe even 15 or 20 percent?*

   Be willing and eager to set uncomfortable giving goals for yourself. That's where God will grow you. Look at what you gave in the last year and say, *I gave X last year, so I am going to stretch myself to give X+Y this year.* As Paul wrote,

   > You must each decide in your heart how much to give. And don't give reluctantly or in response to pressure. "For God loves a person who gives cheerfully." (2 Cor. 9:7)

2. **A desire to be generous with others:** When you see needs around you, you are quick to help. Rather than debating with yourself over whether you should help, you

automatically give to the need. Being able to live in a place of quick generosity shows that you are controlling your money, not the other way around.

3. **A decision to fully use your income to accomplish God's purposes in the world:** By the way, we stole that phrase directly from the Bible. In a letter to Philemon, a Christian living in Colossae, Paul wrote,

> And I am praying that you will put into action the generosity that comes from your faith as you understand and experience all the good things we have in Christ. (Philem. 1:6)

The only way to fully understand the power of the Generosity Secret is to grow beyond obedience-level giving and step into the realm of extravagant generosity. Scripture makes this promise:

> Remember this: Whoever sows sparingly will also reap sparingly, and whoever sows generously will also reap generously. (2 Cor. 9:6 NIV)

Think about the people around you. Who in your life has modeled this kind of openhanded generosity for you? Who has excelled in the grace of giving at this level? If you can't think of anyone, then God may be calling you to set a new example among your friends and relatives. Will you be the one to fully embrace the Generosity Secret and encourage others to do the same?

I (Nelson) have been fortunate in my life to have been around some people who epitomize these three characteristics of generous living. I've seen what generosity has done in their lives, and it has motivated me to continually stretch myself.

One early mentor and friend of mine, in particular, has been an inspiration for generous living. He wrote a book that became a bestselling title far beyond any expectation and beyond his wildest dreams. When he was in the process of writing, he thought he was just working on a little book that would help people reorient their lives toward the purposes of God. But God had other plans.

The unbelievable sales of his book brought incredible financial reward. When my friend got his first royalty check, which was quite large, I asked him, "What are you going to do with all of the money this book is generating?" He answered, "I'm not sure yet, but I am searching the Scripture to see what God would have me do."

Not too many weeks later, he called me and said, "I have decided to do four things. Number one, I've decided not to change my lifestyle. In other words, I'm not going to sell the house I've lived in for twenty years and buy a place in Malibu. I'm not going to sell my ten-year-old Ford and get a limousine. I'm going to keep my lifestyle the way it is."

"Secondly," he continued, "I am going to set up two foundations. One to help hurting pastors around the world and the other to help hurting children who have been orphaned by the HIV/AIDS pandemic. Thirdly, I have decided to pay back to my church all of the salary I've earned as their pastor for the last twenty years and continue pastoring for no income."

Needless to say, I was already so shocked by these first three decisions that I couldn't imagine what the fourth was going to be.

"Finally, I have decided to become a reverse tither." I honestly didn't know what he meant.

He explained, "The Bible says you are supposed to bring 10 percent of your income back to God and live on 90 percent. I'm going to flip it. I am going to bring 90 percent of my income back to God and live on 10 percent."

Talk about someone whose story challenges all of us to be generous givers! You may not be able to be a reverse tither, but maybe you could whittle away at that 90 percent. What is God calling you to? Part of committing to a life of generosity means asking these questions and allowing ourselves to be stretched and used by God.

But wait, there's more. As Paul Harvey would say, "And now, the rest of the story . . ."

When my friend and his wife married over twenty years ago, they made a decision to excel in the grace of giving. They embraced the Generosity Secret, set on living their lives under the canopy of God's blessing. What did that look like? Well, tithing was a no-brainer for them—a minimum command—so as soon as they were married, they started stretching themselves by giving an extra percent every year.

The first year of their marriage, they gave 11 percent. The second year, they gave 12 percent. The third year, 13 percent, and so on. Now, these weren't wealthy people. At the time, my friend was a struggling young pastor just out of school. He didn't have much money. The yearly increase was always a huge step of faith. But it's one he wanted to take, based on the truth and promises of God's Word.

Through the years, my friend's openhanded living had shown God that he could be trusted with worldly wealth. He had demonstrated that his heart was not tied to his money.

He had learned to truly excel at giving. And then God chose him to write a bestselling book that has influenced the entire world.

I've heard my friend say, "I'm not surprised that God wanted the message of this book to get out there; I'm just surprised he chose me to write it." I'm not. God chose him because he had shown that he could be trusted with the inevitable, impending success. He had proven himself to be a faithful, generous giver.

Now, you are probably not going to write the next bestseller. Neither am I. Odds are that you and I are not in danger of having millions and millions of dollars flood into our lives. But isn't that a great model, no matter what our level of income is?

Ask the Lord, "God, how can I be a generous giver right now? How can I best honor you with my financial life? What are you calling me to?" Maybe you need to take the step of increasing your giving by a percentage every year. Maybe you can decide to consistently help people who are in need. You have the freedom to make those kinds of decisions when you choose to live a life that fully embraces the Generosity Secret.

One of the easiest traps you can fall into is to tell yourself that you will give more when you have more. That's just not true. Unless you learn to be generous with the resources that are in your life right now, you will not be generous with your resources later on. It's quite a bit harder to give 10, 11, or 12 percent of $200,000 than it is to give the same percentage of $20,000. You do the math.

If you don't start with the $20,000, your money will only make its way further into your heart as it increases. Remember our original paradigm shift: Your money is not yours.

You are just a manager. God doesn't give you increase so you can be more comfortable or advance your lifestyle. He gives you more so you can give more. You are his conduit.

Generous Giving = Generous Living

Giving generously doesn't have anything to do with the actual dollar amount you give; it has everything to do with what that dollar amount is in proportion to your income. When you quickly and cheerfully give over and above the minimum requirement, you are a generous giver, no matter where the decimal point falls.

One day, Jesus decided to go to the temple to watch as people dropped their money into the offering box. Contrary to common assumptions, he wasn't too impressed with the rich people who put in the large gifts. Let's look at how the story unfolds:

> Jesus sat down near the collection box in the Temple and watched as the crowds dropped in their money. Many rich people put in large amounts. Then a poor widow came and dropped in two small coins.
>
> Jesus called his disciples to him and said, "I tell you the truth, this poor widow has given more than all the others who are making contributions. For they gave a tiny part of their surplus, but she, poor as she is, has given everything she had to live on." (Mark 12:41–44)

Whether you can best relate to this old widow or to the likes of Bill Gates, you are called to be a generous giver right now, in your current circumstance. As you take that step, you will be stepping into a life blessed beyond your wildest imagination. A world you never knew existed will be fully within your reach. Remember, you were created to give. Doing so is the air that allows you to soar.

> But those who trust in the LORD will find new strength.
> They will soar high on wings like eagles. (Isa. 40:31)

The Top Five Ways to Invest Your Treasure

1. Give a full 10 percent.

- "A tenth of all you produce is the LORD's, and it is holy" (Lev. 27:30).
- "Yes, you should tithe, and you shouldn't leave the more important things undone either" (Matt. 23:23).

2. Give extravagantly.

- Read about how Jesus receives and praises an extravagant gift in Matthew 26:6–13.
- "I assure you, wherever the Good News is preached throughout the world, this woman's deed will be talked about in her memory" (Matt. 26:13).

3. Give sacrificially.

- "He will give you all you need from day to day if you live for him and make the Kingdom of God your primary concern" (Matt. 6:33).
- "They gave as much as they were able, and even beyond their ability. Entirely on their own, they urgently pleaded with us for the privilege of sharing in this service" (2 Cor. 8:3–4).

How much will I commit to give extravagantly/sacrificially over the next twelve months?

- _____ percent above my regular tithes and offerings, or
- $ _____ above my regular tithes and offerings.

4. Give cheerfully.

- "I want you to be leaders also in the spirit of cheerful giving. . . . This is one way to prove that your love is real, that it goes beyond mere words" (2 Cor. 8:7–8).
- "Each one should give what he has decided in his heart to give, not reluctantly or under pressure" (2 Cor. 9:7).

5. Invest in and live for eternity.

"Don't store up treasures here on earth, where moths eat them and rust destroys them, and where thieves break in and steal. Store your treasures in heaven, where moths and rust cannot destroy, and thieves do not break in and steal. Wherever your treasure is, there the desires of your heart will also be" (Matt. 6:19–21).

Part 4

Peace, Influence, and Eternal Impact

Moving beyond Your Limiting Beliefs

How to Silence the Misguided Financial Voices in Your Head

> GENEROSITY SECRET:
> **Your dominating thoughts about money create your financial reality.**

May the words of my mouth
  and the meditation of my heart
be pleasing to you,
  O Lord, my rock and my redeemer.
                    Psalm 19:14

There are not many country songs about having a lot of money. Being the huge country-music fan I (Nelson) am, I have taken inventory. There are a few classics, like "If You've Got the Money, I've Got the Time" and several others about adult beverages and money, but most that mention money focus on not having enough of it. These songs echo a mindset about struggle and lack that is pervasive in a large percentage of people. Maybe that's why I grew up loving country music; I grew up in a home without much money.

My dad was raised by his grandparents after being orphaned by his birth parents. He grew up on what we would today call a self-sustaining farm. By that I mean that if they needed it, they raised it, grew it, made it, or otherwise figured out how to get it from the farm. He used an outhouse into his teenage years and hand pumped water from the outside well. He was lucky a bus stop was added within walking distance of the farm or he would have been homeschooled. In short, he grew up extremely poor. So did my mom.

My parents met and married young, intent on carving out a better life. My father did what many young men did in the 1950s: he joined the military. During his service, he learned how to work on automobiles, which led to him opening a private auto shop under the shade tree in the back of my parents' first home after his discharge. Slowly, my mom and dad advanced from poor to slightly above poor. My dad grew his auto shop from its base under that shade tree to a rented garage bay by the time I was born. Growing up, I didn't have to use an outhouse, but I did share a bathroom with three brothers. I also had to earn any money I needed beyond school lunch money—$1.25 back in my day. Throughout my childhood and early teen years, my dad continued to work hard and build his business. When he finally retired, he owned his own multi-bay garage and my family could officially be deemed middle class.

My family was never greedy, but I wouldn't say we were generous either. Since church was on the far peripheral of our everyday life, I wasn't taught about giving or tithing (although my mom did always make sure I put something in the offering plate when she took me to Vacation Bible School or when we went to the occasional revival service). There were no books about money lying around our house. We lived month to month; we didn't know any other way existed. Throughout my growing-up years, I often heard many of the common lower-economic proverbs about the lack of money trees in our backyard, how money doesn't buy happiness, that rich people can't be trusted, or (my favorite misquoted Bible verse) that money is evil.

On the more positive side, my parents both worked hard. My dad saved and invested—first in his own shop and then in other rental / income-producing properties. My mom went to work in the public school system as soon as my brothers and I were old enough to be somewhat independent, and she worked hard to secure her retirement and long-term insurance. My parents avoided all debt except a simple mortgage. They provided for their family and enjoyed life but always on a tight budget.

Why tell you all of this? Maybe it explains my appreciation for country music. My dad loved all the songs about hard work, living on love, and not enough money at the end of the month. Beyond that, it illustrates how I grew up with both good and bad messages about money saturating my subconscious—just as I bet you did, whether your family was wealthy or not so wealthy.

In order to move to a new level of financial awareness, I had to get rid of some "stinking thinking"—to quote the late

Zig Ziglar—that I had acquired about money while I was growing up. I've had to let go of some of my parents' wrong mindsets about money that were second nature to me. I've had to do some head work regarding finances to make sure my internal dialogue lines up with biblical truth.

How about you? What beliefs about money did you inherit from your parents or the culture you grew up in? Do those beliefs reflect the truth of what we have covered in these pages? Or do they stand in opposition, serving only to hold you back? Do you need to work through some ingrained misconceptions and mental roadblocks that may be keeping you from the financial life you want?

Talking to Yourself about Money

Go to any metropolitan city in the world and you will inevitably see someone walking down the street talking to him- or herself. Your tendency, like most people, is probably to pity that person for being disturbed as you watch their one-sided conversation out of the corner of your eye. The irony is that you carry on conversations with yourself all the time too. We all do—just not usually out loud. You may not even realize you are doing it. But whether you're aware of it or not, you talk to yourself all day every day through the thoughts you allow to consume your mind.

Even if you have never keyed in to them, your conscious and subconscious thoughts are your constant companions. They drive and form your every waking moment. How you choose to direct your thoughts in every area will ultimately define your life. As James Allen writes on this topic in the classic work *As a Man Thinketh*:

Man is made or unmade by himself; in the armory of thought he forges the weapons by which he destroys himself; he also fashions the tools with which he builds for himself heavenly mansions of joy and strength and peace. By the right choice and true application of thought, man ascends to the Divine Perfection; by the abuse and wrong application of thought, he descends below the level of the beast. Between these two extremes are all the grades of character, and man is their maker and master.[1]

You are made or unmade by your thoughts. This is as true for your finances as any other area of your life. Day after day, month after month, and year after year, your thoughts create the condition of your life. So much so that situations and circumstances you perceive as happening *to* you are usually happening *because of* you in one way or another. That's a tough pill to swallow, isn't it? No matter what the current state of your finances may be, your cumulative thoughts and subconscious beliefs have helped to land you there. And every day, they either keep you where you are, pull you backward, or propel you into a better future.

> "What you see and what you hear depends a great deal on where you are standing. It also depends on what sort of person you are."
> —C. S. Lewis

The good news is that you get to choose whether what goes on in your head works for or against you. You have the capacity to maximize the thoughts that are beneficial to your finances and every other area of your life, and to disregard those that would try to keep you from attaining the full measure of what God has for you. This powerful reality has been co-opted and skewed in the past by nonbiblical thinkers, but, in its original form, it is God's idea. He not only gives us the power to control our thoughts and to use them to cooperate with his plan for us but also tells us to do just that, as we'll see later in this chapter.

Your dominating thoughts about money create your financial reality. How? First, they fashion your beliefs about finances. Valid or not, those beliefs shape your attitudes about yourself and your relationship with money. Your attitudes create your feelings, and your feelings drive the actions you take every day.[2] The way you see yourself and the world around you is an outgrowth of what goes on in your mind. Everything you choose to do or not do starts with the seed of thought. As such, getting a handle on your internal dialogue about money, its purpose, its availability, and your relationship with it is nonnegotiable when it comes to creating the life you are meant to live.

Growing the Good

Have you ever taken the idea of sowing and reaping to heart? I'm sure you've heard it said, "You will reap what you sow." Yes, it's a farming principle—your harvest will be the result of the type and quality of the seeds you plant—but only on the surface. The truth of sowing and reaping applies to every area of life. When it comes to the words that fill your mind, this principle can make or break you. Writing to the church in Galatia, Paul describes its unavoidability:

Don't be misled: *No one makes a fool of God. What a person plants, he will harvest.* The person who plants selfishness, ignoring the needs of others—ignoring God!—harvests a crop of weeds. All he'll have to show for his life is weeds! But the one who plants in response to God, letting God's Spirit do the growth work in him, harvests a crop of real life, eternal life. (Gal. 6:7–8 MSG, emphasis added)

Every one of your thoughts is a seed that will eventually reap a harvest. What kind of harvest that is will be determined by what kind of seeds you sow. The very life you live is the bounty of your thoughts—its makeup completely determined by what you choose to plant.

The thoughts you think act as instructions to your brain; as soon as they come through, your brain goes to work to turn them into reality. Or in keeping with the planting analogy, when you plant seeds of thought—no matter what kind of seeds they are—your brain gets busy producing a corresponding crop. Your subconscious mind can't differentiate between useful seeds and weed-producing seeds or between what's true and beneficial to you and what's not. It simply keys in to the thoughts running around in your head, takes them at face value, and begins the process of growing them. That being the case, you need to step back and think about what you are saying to yourself in your ongoing internal conversations about money.

Thinking about Thoughts

Since the quality of your life—in every area, not just financially—is so directly tied to the quality of your internal dialogue, you must do what you can to shape that dialogue for your best interests. It's not enough just to understand the power of your thoughts or to know you need to change. You have to take specific action. Thankfully, there are three practical steps you can take to help you adopt consistently better thinking:

1. **Listen to your internal dialogue.** The first step to creating a healthier thought life doesn't require you to do anything but listen. Become aware of the script that's constantly running in your own head. When you talk to yourself about your finances, your ability to make money, or your needs and wants, listen to what you are saying.

   One of the main things that separates us from animals is our ability to think about our thought life; to note an individual thought passing through our mind, analyze it for its truth and worth, and then act on it accordingly. God gave us that unique ability when he made us in his image. But, so often, we let our thoughts run on autopilot. They come from the poor seeds planted in us as we were growing up or spring from the remnants of bad financial situations we've faced. They are just there, and we don't give much consideration to exactly why they are there. Or worse, we forget that we are the masters of our own thoughts and let them have their way with us. As you begin tuning in to your own mental environment, keep these basic truths about thoughts in mind:

   - You can't always control the thoughts that come into your mind. Wrong thinking can and will show up for any number of reasons. While you can't always keep untrue thoughts from pinging you, you can control what you do with them.

- Thoughts have only as much power as you give them. The more you dwell on a certain thought, the more powerful it will become in your life.

Becoming aware of what's going on in your head is key to changing it for the better—but it's just the first step. Next, you have to take some directed action in response to what you hear.

2. **Take every thought captive.** When you accept Jesus's free gift of salvation and place your trust in him (as we discussed in chapter 4), he begins to change you from the inside out—but you have to cooperate with what he's doing by taking an active role in directing your mind toward things that align with his truth. As God begins to fill you with more peace, love, and joy, the effects of those gifts will be thwarted if you refuse to let them take root and influence your thoughts. It's up to you to resist habitual thought patterns and instead match your brain to the new thing God is doing in your spirit. How? By taking two steps Paul outlined in his letters to early Christian believers. The first step is to take every thought captive:

> Take captive every thought to make it obedient to Christ. (2 Cor. 10:5 NIV)

This starts with listening to the thoughts in your head, but it goes further. You have to evaluate your thoughts, trapping and disposing of the ones that don't line up with God's truth. Secondly, Paul says to do this:

> Fix your thoughts on what is true, and honorable, and right, and pure, and lovely, and admirable. Think about things that are excellent and worthy of praise. (Phil. 4:8)

Paul says to *fix your thoughts*. In other words, be proactive in choosing how you focus your thoughts. When you capture and get rid of *stinking thinking* that is not in line with what God wants to do in your life and then follow that up by shifting your attention to things that are true, right, and excellent, you will begin to see yourself and the world around you differently. Your self-image will improve. Your financial life will take a turn for the better. And that's before words even begin coming out of your mouth.

There's one more key ingredient to making this shift—something that has to happen in the space between these two steps, causing them to work together to become a lifestyle rather than just a short-term fix.

3. **Replace old thinking with new.** Psychologists tell us that you can't just get rid of a bad habit, including a negative thought pattern. You have to fill the vacated space with something new. Otherwise, your well-intentioned change won't last; you'll revert right back to listening to the familiar voices in your head. So, as you begin eliminating the ingrained thoughts that don't benefit you financially, you have to immediately replace those thoughts with new ones that do. As you ship out the internal dialogue that keeps you bound,

immediately fill the space in your mind that those thoughts occupied with a corresponding positive internal dialogue. In other words, be quick to connect truth to the vacated space of your captured thoughts so those old thoughts can't creep back in.

One leading author on the topic describes this concept by viewing the mind as a mental apartment furnished by your thoughts:

[This furniture] is the old negative way of thinking that was handed down to us from our parents, our friends, our teachers. They gave us the furniture which we have kept and which we use in our mental apartment. Now let's say that I agree to come over and help you get rid of all the old furniture. We remove every piece, every dish, every rug, table, bed, sofa and chair. We take out every old negative self-belief and store it away safely out of sight.

After I leave, you stand in the middle of your mental apartment. You look around and think, "This is great! I've gotten rid of all my old negative thinking." . . . A little later that evening, after spending an hour or two with nothing but yourself and an empty apartment, what do you suppose you will do? You will go out to the garage where the old furniture is stored, and get a chair! A little later, you will make another trip to the garage and bring in a table. . . . One by one you will begin to bring your old trusted and time-worn negative thoughts back into your mental apartment! Why? Because when I helped you remove the old furniture I didn't give you any new furniture to replace it with.

> When you decide to stop thinking negatively, and do not have an immediate, new positive vocabulary to replace the old, you will always return to the comfortable, old, negative self-talk of the past.[3]

What false, negative mindsets do you have about your relationship to money? Do you have a sense that you'll never have all you need? Somewhere deep down, do you think you don't deserve to have margin and abundance? When negative, self-defeating thoughts about money pop up, it's not enough to simply say to yourself, "Oh, I know I shouldn't think like that." Instead, you have to shift your focus toward truth. The most effective way to do that is to immediately replace the unproductive thought with a corresponding positive one. Out with the old, in with the new.

For example, if you find yourself thinking something unconstructive like, *Everyone in my family struggles financially, so I guess that's just the way it is,* capture that thought, get rid of it, and then immediately fill the space with a better thought like, *God is doing a new thing in me and through me. He wants to bless me.* Don't just stop at getting rid of the unhealthy thought; if you do, it will come back again and again. Instead, be intentional about putting something new in its place. Maybe you can see yourself in some of these other examples:

Old Thinking: *I need to make more money to be happy.*

Replacement: *I'm so thankful for the income I have and what it provides for me.*

Old Thinking: *Money corrupts people. It's better to have less.*

Replacement: *Money is a tool God wants to give me to be used for his purposes.*

Old Thinking: *I just can't stop spending. I'll never get out of debt.*

Replacement: *I am content with what I have right here, right now.*

Old Thinking: *I'm not talented enough to do what I really want to do.*

Replacement: *I am blessed with incredible skills and abilities, and I use them to their full potential to create the life God has in store for me.*

Old Thinking: *It's greedy to try to earn more.*

Replacement: *I want to earn more so I can give more.*

Old Thinking: *Only the wealthy can be philanthropists.*

Replacement: *Anyone can be generous!*

You aren't being delusional or ignoring reality when you replace your negative thoughts with healthier, positive ones. You are simply choosing to see the other side of the coin; it has been there all along, you just haven't been looking at it. There's more than one way to think about every situation and reality in your life. When you choose to see the positive, you are agreeing with God's perspective—you are agreeing with his view of you and your circumstances. That alone will propel you toward a fuller, happier life. As Paul writes,

> Don't copy the behavior and customs of this world, but *let God transform you into a new person by changing the way you think.* Then you will learn to know God's will for you, which is good and pleasing and perfect. (Rom. 12:2, emphasis added)

There it is. God is in the process of transforming you from the inside out, but he can't complete that work in you unless you let him, unless you cooperate with him by letting his thoughts become your thoughts. Do your part to step out of your old ingrained thinking and fill your mind instead with thoughts that can elevate you to the best, truest version of yourself, making you into a person ready to accept the abundant life God has in store for you (John 10:10). Everything you are, everything you do, and everything you have begins in your mind. Cooperate with God in changing those words first, and your whole life will reflect the change.

CHAPTER 13

What Do You Do?

Trading the Good for the Great in Your Career

—— GENEROSITY SECRET ——
When you align your path with God's plan, you will become truly successful. (True Success = God's Will)

Work willingly at whatever you do, as though you were working for the Lord rather than for people.

Colossians 3:23

You likely started planning your career path from an early age. You had to; from the time you stepped into kindergarten, grown-ups began asking you what you wanted to be when you grew up. So, you formulated an answer. I (Nelson) used to say I wanted to be a lawyer. Then I wised up and changed my answer to astronaut. What about you? What did you want to be? More importantly, do you want to be what you have become?

Most people end up chucking their childhood plans somewhere along the way in favor of a career track that's wiser or more stable than being a rodeo clown. (No offense to rodeo clowns. Or lawyers.) The problem is, too often they allow themselves to get carried along by an erratic stream of monetary needs, personal connections, and random job openings that sound interesting, until they wash up on a shore they never saw coming. They may end up working a decent job but feel frustrated, out of sync, or dissatisfied. Does this ring true for you? If not—if you are happy and fulfilled in your chosen career path and you're making an income that lends itself to your financial freedom as defined in these pages—then congratulations. That's wonderful. You can skip this chapter. But if you feel like your job is a major contributing factor to the financial situation you are hoping to transform, then read on. You may need to make an adjustment that will better align you with God's plan not only for your finances but also for your overall path.

One of the most frustrating positions you can find yourself in is wanting to make a change for financial betterment but feeling like you are stuck in a job that is not providing you with the opportunities or income you may have access to somewhere else. Maybe you simply don't like what you do. Maybe there is no room for upward mobility. Maybe your pay doesn't adequately reflect your effort. Maybe you know you should be doing something else, but you don't know how to get from where you are to where you want to be. If any of these widespread realities resonate with you, step back and evaluate what's going on from two perspectives:

1. Analyze your true **motives** behind the work you do. In other words, what definition of success drives you in the workplace?
2. Examine your personal **makeup** in relation to your career or job situation. How are you uniquely wired, and how does that mesh with the path you are on?

Motives: How Do You Define Success?

Your definition of success will determine not only your overall career path but also your daily performance on the job. If you define success by position, you'll be focused on advancing through the ranks of your company. If you define success by income, you may do whatever it takes, ethically or otherwise, to increase your bottom line. If your definition centers on power, you're likely to manipulate the people and situations around you in an attempt to gain control. If fame is your pinnacle, you'll devise all sorts of plans to get your name spoken around America's dinner tables.

Since your definition of success drives your career—and since you probably spend anywhere from two hundred to four hundred hours working every month—it is safe to say that how you define success will shape your entire life. So, what is success for you? What's your definition? Perhaps more importantly, how do you know if your definition is right? Is there a definitive measure? What if you continue pursuing your vision of success only to get to the end of your life and realize that you were off target all along—that your pursuit was empty?

As with most philosophical questions, Scripture can offer some insight here. First of all, success is not defined by the external measurements of society. Jesus warns,

> Beware! Guard against every kind of greed. Life is not measured by how much you own. (Luke 12:15)

There we are again. Generosity, not greed, is the foundation of a successful life. Even though we all would agree with that truth, we still have an innate tendency to live as though our possessions are some kind of barometer. But as we've covered extensively throughout these pages, Jesus says that's not how life is measured.

Later in the New Testament, Paul gives another clue to tease out the true definition of success:

> It is not that we think we are qualified to do anything on our own. Our qualification comes from God. (2 Cor. 3:5)

The success we attain is from God, not merely from our own efforts. As Paul is saying, success as defined by human standards is a skewed goal. It's not about us; it's not about what we can grasp. True success has a larger, lasting value.

Even though success will look a little different for every individual, there are certain principles that inhabit all authentic achievement. Consider the three questions below. How you answer them is a good indicator of whether you are on the path to true success or whether a professional shift may be in order:

1. Are you serving others?

Ralph Waldo Emerson wrote, "It is one of the most beautiful compensations of life, that no man can sincerely try to help another without helping himself."[1] Emerson understood that helping others is good for your soul. What he may not have realized was that the level to which you are willing to serve other people will determine the level of your ultimate success.

Servant is the word most associated with success in the Bible, but today the word sounds radical. None of us live in a culture that focuses on selfless service. Whether any of us like to admit it or not, our mindset is often one of, "What's in it for me?" Servants, on the other hand, ask, "What can I do for you?" They put other people and their needs before themselves and their own.

Jesus's disciples were also concerned with succeeding. They even debated among themselves about which one of them was the greatest. They competed for recognition and accolades. They each wanted to be the guy to sit at Jesus's right hand in the kingdom of heaven. Jesus was quick to remind them that greatness and success are not about position but about service:

> The greatest among you must be a servant. But those who exalt themselves will be humbled, and those who humble themselves will be exalted. (Matt. 23:11–12)

In your quest for success, it is imperative that you cultivate the ability to humble yourself and serve those around you. Significance isn't found in a salary but in how well you bless other people. Quite simply, God blesses you when you bless others! For deeper study on achieving true greatness through service, see our book *The Greatness Principle: Finding Significance and Joy by Serving Others* (Baker Books, 2012). For specific ideas on how to proactively serve others, go to www.TheGenerositySecret.com.

2. **Are you growing others?**
   Do your friends, family, and coworkers feel encouraged after spending time with you? Do you respect other people enough to want them to reach their full potential? How you answer these questions will let you know how well you are growing others. Whether you realize it or not, you have a basic responsibility to help the people around you become better human beings. As the ancient saying goes, if you treat an individual as he is, he will stay as he is; but if you treat him as if he were what he ought to be and could be, he will become what he ought to be and could be. How well are you helping the people in your life become what they ought to be and could be?

   The best way to grow others is to take Jesus's most important command to heart and live it out in your day-to-day dealings with the people around you, aka your neighbors:

   > "You must love the LORD your God with all your heart, all your soul, and all your mind." This is the first and greatest commandment. A second is equally important: "Love your neighbor as yourself." (Matt. 22:37–39)

When you make the choice to intentionally love God and love your neighbor as yourself, you cultivate good things in the lives of those you love. Plus, as you help others grow, God will grow you:

> Give, and you will receive. Your gift will return to you in full—pressed down, shaken together to make room for more, running over, and poured into your lap. The amount you give will determine the amount you get back. (Luke 6:38)

Take an interest in helping others in your life become better in every area. Show them love when they don't deserve it. Invest in their future. Support them in their spiritual journey. The more generously you give of yourself, the more you will grow—and the closer you will get to true success.

3. **Are you expanding God's plan?**
   Success comes when you are more interested in doing God's will and accomplishing his work than in doing things your own way. That is, when God's plan for your life and for your circle of influence takes the number one slot on your priority list. If you are wondering what God's plan is and how you can make it your top priority, just refer back to questions one and two. God's plan is for you to serve others and help them grow.

   As Thomas Wolfe has been credited with saying, "You have reached the pinnacle of success as soon as you become uninterested in money, compliments or publicity." We would take this assertion a step further and add that true success is knowing you are being obedient to God. When you obey God by making his plan your motivation and then act on that plan by consciously serving others and helping them grow spiritually, he will make you successful in everything you do. If your definition of success is rooted in this truth, you will never have to worry about coming up empty in the end.

Makeup: What Kind of Work Are You Wired For?

Once you have analyzed your motives in the workplace and defined true success, spend some time evaluating your makeup as it relates to your current work situation. In other words, consider how God wired you and how that wiring affects your career.

Gone are the days when people used to work in one profession or for one company for an entire career. In our culture, we are constantly reinventing ourselves. Our professional goals shift and evolve as our overall desires evolve. By taking the time to evaluate what skills, talents, and abilities God gave you and what they are most suited for, you'll be able to choose your career more effectively and avoid some of the painful storms that come from being on a path that doesn't suit who you are. Begin by asking God to show you his wisdom:

> If you need wisdom, ask our generous God, and he will give it to you. He will not rebuke you for asking. (James 1:5)

Then ask yourself these four questions:

1. What does God want?

You've probably come to the realization that life is not about you. God's purposes extend far beyond your personal and financial concerns. So it makes sense to ask yourself—and God—what he wants for your life. After all, he is the One who created you. He chose the parents you were born to, the country you were born in, and the opportunities you had access to. He controls all of these factors because he has a specific plan for your life. Ask him what it is, and then listen for his answer.

As one bestselling author has fervently noted, "Good is the enemy of great."[2] You may be able to do lots of good things with your life, but if you are operating outside of God's will, you won't ever tap into the magnitude of the life he has in store for you, financially or otherwise. If you settle for good, you will miss out on great. God wants you to have the best, most abundant life possible (John 10:10). When you align yourself with his will, you will be able to do just that.

2. What are you good at?

I (Nelson) grew up with a guy named John. John was a great golfer. He was wired for it. He played all through junior high and high school and then went to college on a golf scholarship. After college, he went on to have some success as an amateur. But John soon realized that he couldn't make a living out of the game he loved. So he examined the skill set that he used on the golf course—the analytical way of thinking, the ability to predict outcomes, etc.—and came to the conclusion that many of those skills would translate well into the business world. He decided to get a degree in corporate finance. Now he uses the skills that he was naturally blessed with to run a successful corporation.

God wired you to do something really well. What is that something? Try to find the point where your passion and your profession can cross paths. If you discover that sweet spot, you will be in a career you love for the rest of your life. Does your current work situation align with what you are naturally good at? Does your position allow you to do work you enjoy? Don't waste time doing something God didn't create you for. As Paul says,

> For we are God's masterpiece. He has created us anew in Christ Jesus, so we can do the good things he planned for us long ago. (Eph. 2:10)

3. What is right in front of you?

God may ultimately have a different plan in store for your life, but he has put you where you are today for a reason. You have to be faithful and diligent to do what is in front of you. He will place stepping-stones in your path to get you where you are supposed to go, but only as you do what needs to be done right now. As God says in Ecclesiastes 9:10 (NASB),

> Whatever your hand finds to do, do it with all your might.

Paul echoes this sentiment later in his letter to the Colossian church:

> Work willingly at whatever you do, as though you
> were working for the Lord rather than for people.
> (Col. 3:23)

God may be using your current situation to shape you
into the person you need to be for the future. Whatever
your work is right now, do it as if you were working
directly for God rather than for other people, profit, or
popularity. As you do, he will guide your steps. If you
are faithful in the small things, you'll be given more.

4. **What is your life's service?**

True success is a by-product of service. When you
view your life and your purpose through the lens of
service, the details of your career begin to fall into
the proper perspective. Your life's work doesn't need
to be centered on getting the best job, accomplishing
professional goals, and moving up the ladder but on
continually seeking God's plan for your career and
using that avenue to honor him and love others.

Don't misunderstand: you
can still land your dream job,
strive for your professional
goals, and create lots of income.
The difference is that, even as
you do those things, they will
not be your priority—they will not be the driving factor of your life. Instead, your success, whether small
or great by the world's standards, will be the result of
your service to others. The greatest leaders in every
area of the business world are the greatest servers
and the greatest givers.

> True success is
> a by-product
> of service.

CHAPTER 14

Putting the Big Rocks in Place

Five Keys for Embracing the Generosity Secret Now

> GENEROSITY SECRET
>
> **Make room for what's most important first.**

I will give them hearts that recognize me as the LORD. They will be my people, and I will be their God, for they will return to me wholeheartedly.

Jeremiah 24:7

One muggy late-summer morning, a wise professor stepped into his classroom determined to prove a point to a bunch of sleepy students. Under his arm he carried a big wide-mouthed jar. He made his way to the front of the room and set the jar on his desk. With the students paying little attention, he filled the jar with five big stones. He put in the stones one by one until the jar couldn't hold any more. Then he asked his students, "Is this jar full?" They half-nodded their assertion that it was.

The professor pulled a bucket of pebbles from under his desk. Slowly, he poured the pebbles into the jar. They bounced and settled into the small spaces that had been created between the stones. Once again, the professor asked his students, who were now slightly more awake, "Is this jar full?" They all quietly contended that, yes, of course it was.

The professor proceeded to pull another bucket from beneath his desk—this one filled with fine sand. As the students looked on, he tilted the bucket of sand into the jar. The granules quickly filled in the barely visible cracks and crevices left between the stones and pebbles. This time when asked, "Is this jar full," the class answered with a resounding, "Yes!"

In response to his students' certainty, the professor reached under his desk and brought out a pitcher of water. The students watched in amazement as the professor poured the entire pitcher into the jar.

Now the professor asked a different question, "What was the point of this illustration? What was I trying to teach you through this now-full jar?"

A student in the back called out, "You were showing us that you can always fit more into your life if you really work at it?"

"No, that's not it," the professor answered. "The point is that you have to put the big rocks in first, or you'll never get them in. These five rocks are your top priorities. Carefully consider what they are, get them set, and everything else will fall into place around them."

The Big Rocks

As the professor proved to his class, you have to put what's biggest, or most important in this context, in your jar first. Then the details will fill in around those things. If you don't put the big rocks that make up a life of generosity and financial freedom in place first, the small stuff will become consuming and crowd them out. How exactly does this apply to living a life defined by the Generosity Secret? Let's break it down.

As established, you honor God with your finances through giving—through excelling in generosity and learning to consistently live an openhanded life. When you begin living by the Generosity Secret, there are five big stones that need to be in place in your financial life. These stones will give you solid footing as you move from a life of self-focused financial strain to a life focused on God's purposes:

Stone 1: Decide to Get Out of Debt

As we highlighted at the very beginning of this book, getting out of debt is a process that begins with a decision (chap. 1). Break the cycle of consumerism and realign your heart with God's by deciding to give first (chap. 5). Then decide that you are going to stop the influx of debt in your life. Don't buy anything else you can't pay for, and put together a plan for paying down the debt you already have (chaps. 6–7). Visit www.TheGenerositySecret.com for some practical debt-reduction tools.

Learn to be content with what you have rather than obsessed with always getting more (chap. 8). As Hebrews 13:5 encourages, "Don't love money; be satisfied with what you have. For God has said, 'I will never fail you. I will never abandon you.'"

Stone 2: Determine Your Priorities

Again, financial freedom has very little to do with your income; it has much more to do with your outflow. When you put God first by honoring him with the tithe (chap. 9) and by choosing to live within your means (chap. 6), you will have your financial priorities in order. Now is the time to begin implementing the 70 Percent Principle of Lasting Wealth (chap. 10) if you haven't already.

Stone 3: Discipline Yourself in Small Financial Ways

Luke, a physician who examined everything about the life of Jesus and wrote a detailed account, warns that unless you are faithful in the small things, you won't be trusted to be faithful in large things (Luke 16:10). In light of this truth, begin to discipline yourself in small ways. This will support every aspect of the financial transformation you are pursuing. For example:

- Commit to embracing the Generosity Secret.
- Make the decision to get out of debt, as mentioned above, and stay out!
- Decide to cut back on something in your life, and put that money toward gaining financial freedom. For example, brew your own coffee instead of buying coffee every day. Take your lunch to work instead of going out for lunch. Use the money you save to pay down

your debt, add to your savings, or give to a need.

Small changes have a huge cumulative effect over time.

Stone 4: Become a Generous Giver

Generosity is a way of life. You don't have to wait until you have more margin to adopt the attitude of a generous giver. Practice living an openhanded life each and every day. Not just with your finances but in all areas (chaps. 9 and 11).

Stone 5: Adopt the Habit of Now

Take your next step today. There's always a reason to wait, but procrastination is dangerous. Napoleon Hill once said, "Procrastination is the bad habit of putting off until the day after tomorrow what should have been done the day before yesterday."[1] The only way to break the habit is to do it now! If you don't start today, a year from today you'll wish you had.

Living by the Generosity Secret

When setting out on any adventure, you have to know where you are, where you are going, and what you need to do to get there. Embracing the Generosity Secret as a way of life is nothing if not an adventure. As these pages draw to a close, consider where you are and what you need to do to get where you want to be.

Are you just getting started? Perhaps you have never given a gift before and you are ready to give for the first time. Do you give sporadically, or even regularly, but not proportionally? Then you haven't quite gotten your arms around the Generosity Secret.

Maybe you need to change your limiting assumptions about money. Maybe you are already tithing, but you feel God calling you into excellence. You need to go even deeper. Perhaps you give extravagantly from time to time, but it's not a lifestyle. What is God calling you to? Be honest; God already knows exactly where you are.

When setting out on an adventure, it also helps to have an example ahead of you to look toward. God is the ultimate example of a generous giver. He gave much more than mere money; he gave his Son. The Gospel of John tells the story:

> For this is how God loved the world: He gave his one and only Son, so that everyone who believes in him will not perish but have eternal life. God sent his Son into the world not to judge the world, but to save the world through him.
>
> There is no judgment against anyone who believes in him. But anyone who does not believe in him has already been judged for not believing in God's one and only Son. And the judgment is based on this fact: God's light came into the world, but people loved the darkness more than the light, for their actions were evil. All who do evil hate the light and refuse to go near it for fear their sins will be exposed. (John 3:16–20)

Giving should always be an outgrowth of love. Because God loved all of us, he gave. Because we love him, we give. In 2 Corinthians 8:5, Paul writes, "They gave themselves first of all to the Lord" (NIV).

The effects of your financial decisions will influence every other area of your life and have the potential to last for generations. The only way to truly honor God with your finances is to acknowledge his ownership and embrace a lifestyle of generosity, but in order to fully do that you have to first climb out of the throne of your own life. You have to shift your concentration from the little kingdom of "me and my needs" to the bigger kingdom of God and his purposes. As you begin to embrace and live out the Generosity Secret, not only will your focus on money move from one of greed to one of generosity, but your very purpose for living will move from the temporal to the eternal.

> As you begin to live out the Generosity Secret, not only will your focus on money move from one of greed to one of generosity, but your very purpose for living will move from the temporal to the eternal.

We began this book by talking about a paradigm shift. Everything you have belongs to God; you are just a manager. Let's take that truth even deeper. Everything you are belongs to God. He created you. Then, so you wouldn't have to be separated from him either in this life or in eternity, he sent his Son to die as a covering for your sins. Through Jesus, he made a way for you to have a relationship with him. All you have to do is accept his offer of salvation. If you are ready to learn more about what that means, turn to the last chapter.

CHAPTER 15

Living for Eternity

How to Make Sure You and Your Money Have Eternal Impact

—— GENEROSITY SECRET ——
**Your money is a tool that can
impact lives now and for eternity.**

*I am praying that you will put into action the generosity that
comes from your faith as you understand and experience all
the good things we have in Christ.*

Philemon 1:6

Life is too short and too important to live with the
constant stress and anxiety that come from not fully
honoring God—not just with your finances but with
your entire being. Let us close with one more little paradigm-
shifting thought. Take a look at this:

The dot above represents your life, the number of years you are on this earth. The arrow represents eternity. Compared to eternity, your life is like a fleeting shadow—here today and gone tomorrow. The Bible actually compares our lives to the morning fog—here for a little while and then gone (James 4:14).

An Eternal Perspective

You will spend a lot more time in eternity than you will in this life. While the short-sighted person lives for the dot, the wise person acknowledges and plans for the reality of the arrow. So far, we've talked almost exclusively about your money and even how you can use it to make a difference for eternity. It would be an injustice to end this book without also making sure that if your money is being used for the eternal purposes of God, you, too, are ready for eternity with God. Please seriously consider the next few paragraphs either for the first time or perhaps as another reminder that your soul is really more important than your money.

Close to thirty years after Jesus's crucifixion, the apostle Paul wrote a letter to guide and encourage the Christians in Rome. According to many scholars, this letter—now known as the book of Romans—offers the clearest available presentation of what Christianity is all about. Nestled within its pages, Paul gives a handful of verses that perfectly outline what it means to trust God. Like a how-to guide for understanding Christianity, these verses work together to illustrate the basics of the gospel message. Take a look:

Romans 3:23: For everyone has sinned; we all fall short of God's glorious standard.

Romans 6:23: For the wages of sin is death, but the free gift of God is eternal life through Christ Jesus our Lord.

Romans 5:8: But God showed his great love for us by sending Christ to die for us while we were still sinners.

Romans 10:9–10: If you openly declare that Jesus is Lord and believe in your heart that God raised him from the dead, you will be saved. For it is by believing in your heart that you are made right with God, and it is by openly declaring your faith that you are saved.

Romans 10:13: For "Everyone who calls on the name of the Lord will be saved."

These verses, taken together, are often referred to as the Romans Road to Salvation.

Think of the individual Romans Road verses as a series of guideposts. Each verse serves as a marker along the road, directing you down the path of biblical truth concerning God's plan for his relationship with you now and for eternity. Start at guidepost 1.

Guidepost 1: Romans 3:23

For everyone has sinned; we all fall short of God's glorious standard.

Paul offers a clear reminder that every living human being has sinned. No one can live up to God's standard of holiness through sheer effort. Being good is not good enough. By its very nature, the sin that exists in your life separates you from God.

Guidepost 2: Romans 6:23

For the wages of sin is death, but the free gift of God is eternal life through Christ Jesus our Lord.

Sin carries a hefty penalty: death. Not only is physical death the result of sin but so is eternal death. When you die without knowing Jesus, you die to the possibility of spending eternity with God in heaven. But the good news of the gospel is that God has provided a way to conquer death. He loves you so much that he sent his Son to pay the wages of your sin.

Guidepost 3: Romans 5:8

But God showed his great love for us by sending Christ to die for us while we were still sinners.

God didn't wait for any of us to act. While we were all still steeped in sin, he provided a way for us to be brought into right relationship with him. He sent his Son to die in our place. Three days after Jesus was crucified, he rose from the grave. His death and resurrection are the lynchpin of the Christian faith.

Guidepost 4: Romans 10:9–10

If you openly declare that Jesus is Lord and believe in your heart that God raised him from the dead, you will be saved. For it is by believing in your heart that you are made right with God, and it is by openly declaring your faith that you are saved.

All you have to do to accept the gift of salvation is believe in your heart that Jesus is the Son of God and confess that belief with your mouth. In other words, ask him to come into your life, forgive you, and be your Lord. If you've never done that, consider saying these words to God right now:

Dear God, I open my heart to you and invite you into my life. I confess that I am a sinner. I ask that you would forgive me of all that I've done wrong. Thank you for sending your Son, Jesus, who died for me and who gives me the opportunity to know you. From this moment on, I want to follow Jesus, in the fellowship of his church. Thank you for accepting me. In Jesus's name I pray. Amen.

When you accept Jesus as your Savior, you can know that your sins have been forgiven and that you will go to heaven when you die.

Guidepost 5: Romans 10:13

For "Everyone who calls on the name of the LORD will be saved."

No matter who you are or what you've done (or not done) in the past, God's promises are for you. If you understand the truths revealed by the five guideposts along the Romans Road, and if you act on them by placing your faith in Jesus, you will receive God's incredible gift of salvation; you will experience a level of living in this world that is possible only when you are under the umbrella of his blessing; and you will be able to face the rest of your days knowing that your eternity in heaven is secure.

If you prayed the prayer above, congratulations! You are now a follower of Jesus. You just made the most important decision of your life. You probably have questions. We've put some resources for you—including a downloadable New Believer's Guide—on our website. Just go to www.TheGen erositySecret.com. Welcome to the journey!

Treasures in Heaven

Consider Jesus's words again:

> Don't store up treasures here on earth, where moths eat them and rust destroys them, and where thieves break in and steal. Store your treasures in heaven, where moths and rust cannot destroy, and thieves do not break in and steal. Wherever your treasure is, there the desires of your heart will also be. (Matt. 6:19–21)

Where your money is, there your heart will be also. Of course, you don't give to earn your salvation; salvation is a free gift from God that can't be earned. But once you realize the full implications of being saved by God's grace, you will be more and more compelled to live a life of staggering generosity dedicated to accomplishing all that God wants to accomplish through you during the time he gives you on this earth.

Your focus will move from your own wants and needs to the plans and decrees of your Father in heaven. You will be continually prompted to give in response to all God has given you. You will want to do more with your money to impact the lives of those around you not only now but for eternity. Here are just a few ideas for how you can make sure you are using your money—and your life—for lasting impact:

- Go on an annual mission trip, either on your own or with your family.
- Pay for someone else to go on a mission trip.
- Support missionaries.
- When you make once- or twice-in-a-lifetime profit, give extravagantly to God—pay off your church's

debt, give to the building program, establish a charitable remainder trust and give it all to missions.

- Should you be on the receiving end of an insurance policy or a will bequest, give the majority for God's purposes.
- When you sell your home to downsize, give the majority to your local church.
- Set a goal to be a reverse tither for the last decade of your life.
- Move to the mission field for a year, and live off the income from your own investments.
- Give generously to your local church or network of churches. While there are many good investments, like education, medicine, and secular nonprofits, the local church is the vehicle God uses to do most of his work in the world.

As you give more and more of your money to God, more and more of your heart will go to God as well. Over time, the subtle bonds of materialism will be completely broken in your life, and you will begin to fully understand and embrace the eternal impact of a life given wholly to God.

At the end of your days on this earth, your relationship with money will be summed up by one of two words—*generosity* or *greed*. You have the opportunity, and now the tools, to make sure that you live a life of true generosity, a life free of stress and anxiety, a life where your needs are met, and ultimately, a life that honors God and furthers his work in the world. You've been given the secret. Now it's your move.

The Generosity Secret

The Generosity Secret is that generosity is the secret.

- Your money is not really your money.
- The most powerful word for financial freedom is *NO*.
- Learning to give leads to financial freedom.
- Giving to God is the first step toward getting out of debt.
- Don't spend your money before you have it.
- Know the facts about your financial life.
- Having more is not the answer.
- Tithing is key to your financial freedom.
- Stop debating the tithe and just test it. You'll know in a few months if it's worth it.
- Tell your money where to go, and you'll never have to wonder where it went.
- You were born to live a generous life.
- Your dominating thoughts about money create your financial reality.
- When you align your path with God's plan, you will become truly successful.
- Make room for what's most important first.
- Your money is a tool that can impact lives now and for eternity.

A Final Note from Nelson and Jennifer

We hope this book will be the beginning of an ongoing conversation. Please visit **www.TheGenerositySecret.com** to connect with us, access many free resources, and share your story.

Notes

Introduction

1. "Personal Finance Statistics: How Do You Compare?," November 25, 2019, http://www.debt.com/statistics.

Chapter 2 A Heart Issue

1. Randy C. Alcorn, *Money, Possessions, and Eternity* (Carol Stream, IL: Tyndale, 2003), 5.

Chapter 3 Owner versus Manager

1. Alcorn, *Money, Possessions, and Eternity*, 8.
2. Alcorn, *Money, Possessions, and Eternity*, 8.

Chapter 4 Just Say No

1. Christy Bieber, "This Is What Americans Regret Spending Money on the Most," *The Motley Fool*, February 23, 2019, https://www.fool.com /personal-finance/2019/02/23/this-is-what-americans-regret-spending -money-on-th.aspx?Cid=U7DYxt.
2. Bieber, "This Is What Americans Regret Spending Money on the Most."
3. C. S. Lewis, *Mere Christianity* (London: MacMillan, 1952), 40–41.

Chapter 5 Opening Your Hand

1. Stephen King, Vassar Commencement Speech, May 20, 2001, http:// www.stephenking.com/news_archive/archive_2001.html.
2. William Carey, quoted on Goodreads, https://www.goodreads.com /author/quotes/396826.William_Carey.

Chapter 6 Down with Debt

1. Dave Ramsey, *The Total Money Makeover* (Nashville: Thomas Nelson, 2003), 19–20.

Chapter 8 Capturing the Contentment Thief

1. "The Clock Thief: A Parable About Contentment," Stories for Preaching, accessed September 30, 2019, https://storiesforpreaching.com /the-clock-thief-a-parable-about-contentment/.

Chapter 9 Hitting Your Stride

1. Alcorn, *Money, Possessions, and Eternity*, 12.
2. Alcorn, *Money, Possessions, and Eternity*, 182.

Chapter 10 The 70 Percent Principle of Lasting Wealth

1. Jim Rohn, *The Art of Exceptional Living* (Wheeling, IL: Nightingale Conant, 1993), 6 compact discs, disc 5, "The Art of Setting Goals."
2. Alcorn, *Money, Possessions, and Eternity*, 328.

Chapter 12 Moving beyond Your Limiting Beliefs

1. James Allen, *As a Man Thinketh* (West Valley City, UT: Waking Lion, 2007), 10.
2. Shad Helmstetter, *What to Say When You Talk to Your Self* (New York: Pocket Books, 1987), 62–71.
3. Helmstetter, *What to Say When You Talk to Your Self*, 85–87.

Chapter 13 What Do You Do?

1. Ralph Waldo Emerson, quoted on Goodreads, https://www.goodreads .com/quotes/29365-it-is-one-of-the-beautiful-compensations-of-life-that.
2. James C. Collins, *Good to Great* (New York: HarperCollins, 2009), 1.

Chapter 14 Putting the Big Rocks in Place

1. Napoleon Hill Foundation, *Napoleon Hill's Positive Action Plan* (New York: Penguin, 1995), 18.

Nelson Searcy is the founding and lead pastor of The Journey Church with locations across New York City and in South Florida. He is the author of many bestselling books, including *The Generosity Ladder*, *Maximize*, *Connect*, *Ignite*, and *Launch*. He is the founder of ChurchLeaderInsights .com and the Renegade Pastors Network. Searcy lives with his wife and son in Boca Raton, Florida.

Jennifer Dykes Henson is a writer, a wife, and a mom to two young girls. She has coauthored several bestselling books, including *The Generosity Ladder* and *The New You*. Previously, Jennifer worked with Dr. Charles Stanley as the marketing communications manager for In Touch Ministries. She lives with her family in Atlanta, Georgia.

Build a small group ministry with
100% participation

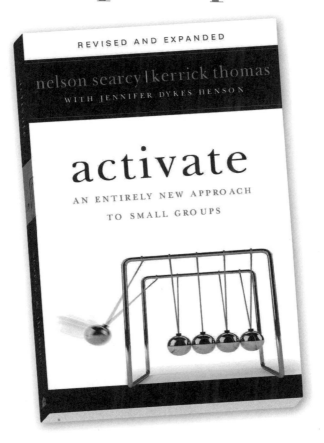

Want to know how to make your small groups work? Drawing from the startling success of small groups at The Journey Church, Nelson Searcy and Kerrick Thomas debunk the myths, set the record straight, and show how you can implement a healthy small group ministry in your church.

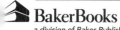

Are you being intentional about your
HEALTH and WELLNESS?

The New You will help you make a decision to stop being carried by the current of bad habits. It takes a holistic view of health that encompasses the physical, mental, emotional, and spiritual areas of your life, giving you proven, systematic ways to dramatically improve each one.